"A lively introduction to the Middle Ages. Fun and educational."
— *School Library Journal*

Knights & Castles

Winner
of the
Children's Book
Council Notable
Book Award,
American Bookseller
Pick of the Lists
Award

A WILLIAMSON *KALEIDOSCOPE KIDS*™ BOOK

DEDICATION

This book is dedicated to the time traveler in you.

ACKNOWLEDGEMENTS

Special thanks to Lady Michelle Begley for her creative contributions and helpful research, and to Master Clayton Mantell for contributing mechanical designs, and Sir Brett Whalen, for eleventh hour clarification.

Williamson Publishing Books by Avery Hart & Paul Mantell:

ANCIENT ROME!
Exploring the Culture, People & Ideas of This Powerful Empire

WHO *REALLY* DISCOVERED AMERICA?
Unraveling the Mystery & Solving the Puzzle

PYRAMIDS!
50 Hands-On Activities to Experience Ancient Egypt

ANCIENT GREECE!
40 Hands-On Activities to Experience This Wondrous Age

BOREDOM BUSTERS!
The Curious Kids' Activity Book

KIDS MAKE MUSIC!
Clapping and Tapping from Bach to Rock

KIDS GARDEN!
The Anytime, Anyplace Guide to Sowing & Growing Fun

Library of Congress Cataloging-in-Publication Data

Hart, Avery.
  Knights & castles: 50 hands-on activities to experience the Middle Ages/ Avery Hart and Paul Mantell.
    p. cm.
  "A kaleidoscope kids book."
  Includes bibliographical references and index. Summary: Introduces the Middle Ages, including activities and crafts that are representative of medieval life, for example, creating an hourglass, a catapult, a coat of arms, and a code of honor.
  ISBN 1-885593-17-1
  1. Civilization, Medieval–Study and teaching (Elementary)–Activity programs– Juvenile literature.   2. Middle Ages–Study and teaching (Elementary)–Activity programs–Juvenile literature. 3. Knights and knighthood–Europe–Study and teaching (Elementary)–Activity programs–Juvenile literature.
  [1. Civilization, Medieval. 2. Middle Ages. 3. Knights and knighthood. 4. Handicraft.] I. Mantell, Paul. II. Title.
  CB351.H24   1998
  940.1–dc21   97-32863
               CIP
               AC

Kaleidoscope Kids® Series Editor: **Susan Williamson**
Cover design: **Joseph Lee Design, Inc.**
Interior design: **Joseph Lee Design, Inc.**
Illustrations: **Michael Kline Illustration**
Printing: **Quebecor Printing, Inc.**

Printed in Canada

Williamson Publishing Co.
P.O. Box 185
Charlotte, Vermont 05445
1-800-234-8791

10 9 8 7

Knights & Castles

50 HANDS-ON ACTIVITIES TO EXPERIENCE THE MIDDLE AGES

Avery Hart & Paul Mantell

Illustrations by
Michael Kline

WILLIAMSON PUBLISHING • CHARLOTTE, VT

Contents

Hear Ye! Hear Ye! Announcing a Magical Invitation

You are hereby invited on a magical journey to the Middle Ages of Europe, time traveling to the early days of knights and castles. To get there, you'll have to go through the "gates of imagination." Through the power of arts, crafts, music, math, feasting, and fantasy, you'll do what kids did then, and more. Along the way, you can compare "Then & Now," to discover how life has changed or stayed the same.

But traveler, be prepared! The Middle Ages were troubled times of extremes and opposites. Like black and white squares on a chessboard, they were years of clashing conflicts, of wonders and horrors. A bold knight might pray for his victim and then chop off his head! Now that's extreme!

You'll discover why the Early Middle Ages used to be called the Dark Ages. Without the bright light of learning, people can make terrible mistakes. Still, good times are part of every period of history, and the kids of the Middle Ages had fun just as you do today! So look for some silly surprises along the way.

Now, pack up your curiosity, and get ready to explore! Soon you'll be making, doing, singing, and playing your way back in time — back to the days of knights and castles!

Setting the Scene

THE MIDDLE OF WHAT?

The Middle Ages (also called medieval times) spanned from 500 AD to 1400 AD. It's the 900 years between the Roman Empire and the Renaissance (REN-ah-sahns), or re-birth, that led to our modern era. We're headed straight for the middle, the Middle Ages, that is!

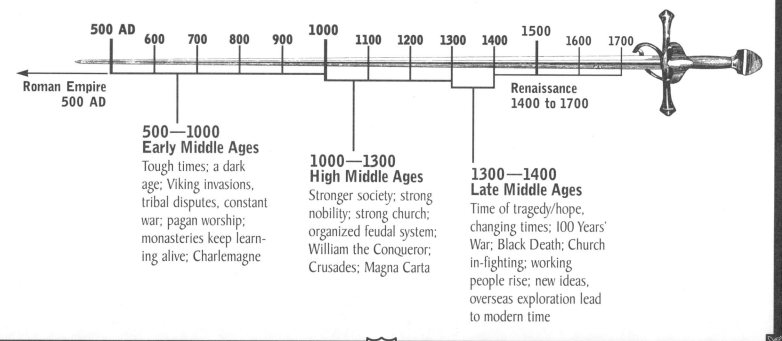

500 AD 600 700 800 900 1000 1100 1200 1300 1400 1500 1600 1700

Roman Empire
500 AD

Renaissance
1400 to 1700

500—1000
Early Middle Ages
Tough times; a dark age; Viking invasions, tribal disputes, constant war; pagan worship; monasteries keep learning alive; Charlemagne

1000—1300
High Middle Ages
Stronger society; strong nobility; strong church; organized feudal system; William the Conqueror; Crusades; Magna Carta

1300—1400
Late Middle Ages
Time of tragedy/hope, changing times; 100 Years' War; Black Death; Church in-fighting; working people rise; new ideas, overseas exploration lead to modern time

GOING TO EXTREMES

The difference between ideals (the way people *wish* things are) and *reality* (the way things really are) was truly extreme in the days of knights and castles. People had conflicting ideas and beliefs about heaven and hell, God and the devil, life and death, wealth and poverty, and what it meant to be a good person.

They thought that God was all-powerful, for instance, but they also believed the devil could harm them. They loved riches and finery, but thought that being poor was a way to be holy. They believed that people should be kind, but often treated others cruelly. To be good Christians, they sometimes went looking for non-Christians — to kill them!

Think About It:

Do you think that everything in our world is "black and white" (all one way or the other)? Or, are there many ways to think about ideas, people, and events (shades of gray)?

A Disappearing Act: "Poof, Begone!"

To travel to the past, you've got to be able to make things vanish. How many objects in your home or school did not exist back in medieval times? How many are in the room where you are reading this book? Look around, and find an item that did not exist back then, point to it, and say, "Poof, Begone!"

If an object wasn't around a thousand years ago, it has to go! Obviously, you'll need to take out cars, airplanes, leaf blowers, fax machines, and TV. See any plastic?

THINK ABOUT TIME

Imagine living without clocks or wristwatches, as people did in medieval times. The passage of time was noted by the movement of the sun, moon, and seasons. The only alarm clock was a bell or the local rooster!

Years and even centuries (every hundred years) seemed to pass with little change. There were few inventions to improve the way people lived.

Today, inventions, discoveries, and technology are continually changing our world. The idea of time moving slowly can be hard for us to understand.

What do you think it was like to live without clocks? There must have been a lot of confusion, but there were probably fewer pressures, too.

Make it disappear, and replace it in your imagination with the materials of the Middle Ages — wood, metal, or stone. Books were rare back then, too, but don't make this one disappear; you need it for more exploration!

Keep wax candles and glass. They were part of the Middle Ages' scene. And if you see a bell, keep it, too. Bells were important a thousand years ago, used to wake people up, mark time, and warn of invaders.

Make a Sandy Hourglass

Medieval clocks, called hourglasses, measured time with trickling sand. (Our modern version of this medieval tool is a three-minute egg timer.)

Your sand timer won't measure an hour, but it will be dependable, because sand always falls at the same speed. Double the time by flipping the hourglass over.

YOU WILL NEED:

✤ **2 equal-sized salad dressing bottles (wide on the bottom, narrow on top) with shaker tops (little holes)**
✤ **Enough sand to fill one bottle**
✤ **A piece of wide, clear postal tape**
✤ **A watch or clock with a second hand**
✤ **A small funnel or piece of cardboard to fill one bottle**

Step 1: Eat a lot of salad so the bottles are available!

Step 2: Remove the labels and the shaker tops, and wash and dry the bottles. To keep in the spirit of the Middle Ages, blow into the bottles to dry them.

Step 3: Fill one bottle with sand. Then, tape the other bottle to it upside down, so the necks are joined.

To time your hourglass, wait until the second hand on your modern clock or watch comes to 12. Then flip the sand clock over. Notice how long it takes for all the sand to fall into the other bottle. (The timer we made from 8 oz./250 ml dressing bottles measures exactly 1 minute and 55 seconds.)

Then & Now

Have you ever been to a place without cars where you had to depend on your own two feet to get around? The fastest speed for traveling in medieval times was the speed of the fastest horse! And not many people got to ride horses, either; they were only for the wealthy. What would be gained, and what would be lost, in a world without modern transportation?

Picture This!

If you walk on a sidewalk, take a moment to think about that modern-day luxury. During the Middle Ages, the only paved roads were those left by the Romans. All others were dirt paths, dusty in summer, muddy in spring, and frozen in winter.

Turn off the Lights!

To get an idea of life during the Early Middle Ages, imagine a dark room. Or better yet, turn off the lights or close your eyes.

In the dark, useful objects are hidden and hard to find. Things that are familiar, like a tree branch waving in the breeze, may seem scary.

During the Early Middle Ages, it was as if all the lights of society were turned off at once! Useful ideas were hidden or hard to find, and new ideas seemed frightening and dangerous to many people!

EUROPE IN THE MIDDLE AGES

In medieval Europe, there were no countries as we know them today. Instead, there were "fiefdoms," large tracts (pieces) of land owned by powerful men or the Church.

Most medieval people lived in one place their entire lives. They could only imagine what the rest of the world was like.

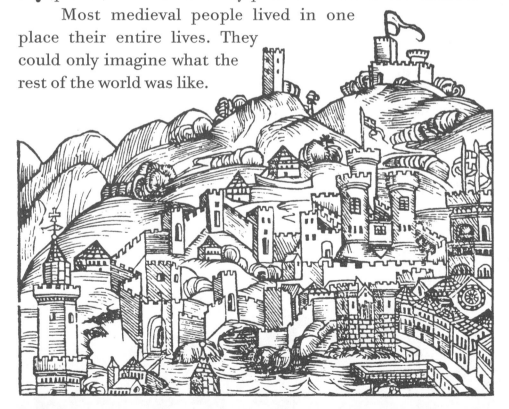

Make a Map

Draw a Middle Ages-style map of your world today, putting in places that are important to you.

Since your map is in the medieval style, imagination and fantasy are allowed! One way to start is to put yourself in the center, with all the familiar places and people around you. Or how about drawing a map of your yard, your block, your town, or even the whole world? Add directions in the lower corner of your map — north, east, south, and west.

Draw first, and then check out a printed map and compare the differences.

Then & Now

Look in an atlas for a map of Europe in 1000 AD; then, look at a map or globe of Europe as it appears today. How have the boundaries in Europe changed over the past 1,000 years?

BOXED IN

Great and advanced civilizations existed in Africa and Asia during medieval times. But the part of the world we call Europe had little to do with them. And for good reason.

Robbers blocked the old "Silk Road" leading east. That was the route the Romans had used to get to Cathay (our modern-day China) for their beautiful silks and satins.

Bandits also stopped travelers heading south to the wondrous African city of Timbuktu (in modern-day Mali). Vikings and Norsemen (in modern Scandinavia) blocked passage to the north. And the mighty Atlantic Ocean blocked the west. Since many Europeans thought the world was flat, they feared they'd fall off the edge if they sailed too far out!

With routes from the north, south, east, and west blocked, no wonder Europe was isolated.

Then & Now
The United Nations in Your Room

In early medieval times, people seldom left their neighborhoods. By the late Middle Ages, they were roving far and wide. Their explorations continue today, as people around the globe trade and communicate with each other. Do you sometimes "talk" to kids around the world on the Internet? Do you own clothing and products made in other countries? Check tags to find out where your possessions come from.

Of course, it's not just material goods that come from around the world. Traditions, foods, ideas — and best of all — friends from other places make life richer and more interesting!

Early medieval people sure missed a lot by keeping their world so small.

How It All Began

A MIX OF PEOPLES

Before Rome, the native people of Europe were Celts (selts), and other tribes, like Vandals, Franks, Angles, Saxons, (old) Germans. Some lived in northeast Europe, across the Rhine River, in a forest wilderness that Rome could not conquer. Some were nomads, roving from place to place.

Druids (DROO-ids) were Celtic priests and judges, who worshipped nature, above all. To them, water, stone, and trees were sacred. They honored women as well as men.

To the Romans, all the tribes, and the Druids, were lowly "barbarians," — uncivilized, primitive people. Rome changed tribal ways by creating land ownership and written laws.

When Roman Emperor, Constantine, became a Catholic (a Christian), in about 320, he wanted everyone else to join the Church, too. He had churches built on sacred Druid places, and discouraged tribal worship.

The mix of Romans, tribal people, Druids, Celts, and Christians — with all their different beliefs — made the Middle Ages a fascinating time.

HOW KNIGHTS AND CASTLES CAME TO BE

The fall of the Roman Empire, when Rome was invaded by tribal Visogoths, was a mighty thunk! With Rome gone, everything fell apart. Tribal chiefs began battling for land, wealth, and power. Over time, these warlords gave themselves titles, like duke, earl, marquis (mar-KEE), and baron. They all called themselves *nobles.* The mightiest of them became kings.

These rulers built fortresses, called castles, to show their power. Inside the castle walls, a whole community of people lived and worked like bees, serving the noble family.

Knights were soldiers on horseback, the fighting forces of the powerful lords. For their skill in warfare, knights were paid in money and land.

Without Rome, many common people went back to their old tribal ways, worshipping as pagans, or non-Christians. The Church had to fight for influence.

And so, the battles were on — Christian vs. pagan, lord vs. lord! Attack and revenge became a way of life that lasted for hundreds of years.

The Code of Chivalry

At the start of the Middle Ages, there was no government to stop the fighting. Every lord made his own laws, ruling by the swords of his knights!

When this situation got out of hand, a set of rules was developed for all knights, called the Code of Chivalry (from the French word for horse, *cheval*).

Some of the rules were good: Knights were supposed to protect people and be kind. But at the opposite extreme, a knight was to show no mercy to non-Christians.

Make Up a Code of Honor

O wise one, you who can write and know the ways of the future, what if the nobles and the people come to you to ask for a Code of Honor? What guidance can you give them? What rules will keep the peace, at home, in school, and in all the land? Write your own Code of Honor.

Roll your Code into a royal scroll, and tie it with a red ribbon. Have a herald stand and announce it to the people (your family or schoolmates).

Think About It:

During the Middle Ages, tolerance, which is respecting the rights of other people to believe as they will, was missing in action! Think if you weren't allowed to go to church, synagogue, temple, or meeting room. Imagine if saying prayers or meditating was illegal. Do you think everyone should be the same religion? Or is there more than one way to think about God?

Picture This!

Hark, the Herald!

Imagine turning on the news and hearing the newscaster shout out the day's events at the top of his or her lungs. Without microphones, people in the Middle Ages had to yell to be heard!

Messengers, known as heralds, would stand on the church or cathedral steps and loudly proclaim the latest announcements. Often, they would tell the common people to get ready for the visit of some noble or other important person. To this day, we call this "heralding someone's arrival."

KING ARTHUR, MERLIN, AND CAMELOT

Picture a kingdom where the weather is always fair and sunny, where snow comes just once a year, and flowers bloom every day. In this happy land, the king is kind and the people are content.

That ideal place could be the castle Camelot (CAM-e-lot), where King Arthur supposedly reigned. His mage (MAYJ), or wise magician, and advisor was the Druid sorcerer Merlin.

No one knows for sure if Arthur actually lived, but many think he did. Whatever is true, King Arthur has come to represent the ideal of chivalry.

Make Up Your Own Legend

Legends, or old stories, about life in Camelot have been passed down throughout history, as poems, stories, songs, and plays. How about making up a King Arthur legend of your own?

If you do, you will be joining a long list of writers that includes the English poet William Wordsworth in the late 1700s going all the way to the writers at Walt Disney Studios today! (Their version of King Arthur's legend is called The Sword in the Stone.*)*

Here's a cast of characters to include:

King Arthur, a gentle and kindly king
Merlin, a wise magician
Lancelot, a brash young knight
Percival, a gentle young knight
Mordrid, Arthur's evil relative
Queen Guinevere, Arthur's beautiful wife

THE ROUND TABLE

King Arthur had a large, round table built for discussions with his knights. The round shape was chosen to show that every knight, and even the king himself, had equal worth. The message of a circle anywhere is: We're all here, and we all count.

Questions Questions

When you are in class at school, do you sit in rows or in a circle? Do you think the people in the back row participate in discussion as much as those in the front row? Do you think sitting in a circle makes people feel equally important?

THE OTHER SIDE OF HAPPINESS

Alas, legends of Arthur often end sadly. Arthur's best knight, Sir Lancelot falls in love with Queen Guinevere, and Arthur goes to war against his own knights! Even in the story, there's too big a distance between the *ideal* of perfection, and the *reality* of human imperfection.

Then & Now
Loyalty

Have you ever had a friend who didn't want you to be friends with anyone else? That's the way it was with nobles in medieval times. The ruling lords wanted their knights and vassals (see page 21) to be loyal to them alone.

But knights often wanted the rewards that other nobles might offer. This made for big trouble.

If you were a knight, could you accept gifts from a noble and then do battle against him? Can you be loyal to more than one friend at a time?

CHARLEMAGNE: KING OF THE HOLY ROMAN EMPIRE

King Arthur may or may not have been real, but Charlemagne certainly was. He was the mightiest tribal warlord of his time, the King of the Franks.

On Christmas Eve in the year 800 AD, he was crowned king of what came to be called "The Holy Roman Empire." But Charlemagne's Empire was *not* holy, for his soldiers were

brutal killers. It was *not* Roman, because the Romans were long gone from Europe. And it was *not* an empire, because he ruled only part of Europe.

But never mind all that; by medieval logic, it was still called the Holy Roman Empire!

A TRIBAL CHIEF AT HEART

Even though he was a Christian, King Charlemagne liked some of the old tribal ways. For instance, he liked to wear animal skins instead of cloth. Once he invited some friends to go hunting and told them to wear their best clothes. They showed up in velvet finery and were surprised when Charlemagne arrived in a traditional Frankish sheepskin. He laughed his head off when they got dirty during the hunt, as he only had to brush the dirt off his skins. Later that night, he bragged that the sheepskins were superior because they never had to be washed!

Charlemagne and the Page You Are Reading

Charlemagne was a powerful king, but he could not read or write. Still, he respected education and wanted his people to learn. He told his men to find the greatest teacher in the land and bring him back to Aachen, where Charlemagne lived. They brought him a teacher named Alcuin. Charlemagne liked the humble teacher and gave him a lot of power in the kingdom. And it's a good thing for us that he did! Here's why:

In those days, Latin was written in all capital letters, with no space between the words and no punctuation. This made reading very difficult to learn.

Alcuin came up with the idea of lowercase letters. He also added spaces between the words and punctuation to show the meaning. The words you are reading right this minute were influenced by Alcuin. Without him and Charlemagne you would have to

FIGUREOUTHOWTOREADANDUNDERSTAN
DSENTENCESTHATLOOKEDLIKETHISANDAL
SOFIGUREOUTWHENASENTENCEENDEDO
RBEGANANDWHETHERITWASAQUESTIONO
RASTATEMENT

Charlemagne was the greatest king of the Middle Ages. He helped put a system in place that governed Europe for hundreds of years. It was called the feudal system.

The Feudal System

A PLACE FOR EVERYONE AND EVERYONE IN HIS PLACE

Every age has a way of keeping society organized. In America and Canada, for instance, the system is democracy — every adult citizen has a chance to vote for who will be in charge.

In the Middle Ages, the system was called the feudal system — and people had no vote about anything! As "underlings," people had to obey and pay powerful "overlords."

Everybody, except for a few kings, had someone above him. Overlords were rich because they charged other people, even very poor people, money to live on their land. They were powerful because they had vassals (somewhat like knights) to fight for them.

There was no separation between church and government, either. People had to follow the rules of the Church — no matter what they believed. They also had to follow the rules of the overlord — no matter how unfair! When the laws of Church and lord clashed, people got caught in the middle! For the common people, the Middle Ages was like a game of Simon Says with two Simons calling out different things to do!

PEASANTS AND SERFS

The people at the very bottom of the feudal system were the poorest peasants who slaved their whole life long for their master. They were bought, used, and sold like farm animals, and their children were even called "litters"!

Sometimes (not often, though) a friend or relative would buy the peasant's life back and set him free. Other times, slaves ran away during battle, or escaped to larger cities, but this didn't happen often. The poorest peasants had short, miserable lives.

Most people were serfs, and their lives weren't much better. Serfs worked a piece of the master's land outside the castle walls, in exchange for protection in times of trouble. Serfs could keep some of the food they grew for their families.

JOAN OF ARC

Joan of Arc, a humble French peasant girl, became a brilliant military leader in the fifteenth century. She claimed that voices in her head helped her do battle and led her to victory. Some jealous people were so frightened of her power that

they said she was a witch! They had Joan burned at the stake to stop her military power and strong influence on people.

But others believed she was a holy person and declared her a saint and a heroine. What a dramatic life of extremes!

Who's Missing?

Part of the missing light of the Middle Ages was the absence of input by females! Middle Ages' laws said women had no rights. They were not allowed to own land, and wives had to give all their money to their husbands — whether they wanted to or not. Some life!

The tip-top of the power structure was all male, with very little influence by women. Still, some noble women and working women managed to gain power. That shows that with determined men and women, civilization can move forward even in the most oppressive times.

Then & Now

He-men and Frilly Girls

Males and females are more alike than different. But in the Middle Ages, that time of extremes, the differences between them were extreme, too. Women were supposed to be tender and "ladylike," and men were supposed to be strong and powerful. If a woman felt strong and powerful, she was expected to hide those feelings. If a man felt weak or sad, he had to hide those feelings, too.

Have you ever noticed TV ads for boys' and girls' toys? Do they make boys seem macho and girls seem weak or frilly? Is a girl less feminine if she is strong? Is a boy less masculine if he shows he cares?

Ranking or Linking?

In the feudal system, people were *ranked* higher or lower than each other. The people on top were thought to be more important. They told the others what to do. (Our military setup is a ranking system, too.) Ranking is efficient and simple to understand: Whatever the king says, goes!

In a democracy, all people are valued and *linked* together to make decisions. This system is not as simple as feudalism. A president or prime minister cannot just give an order and expect everyone to obey it! He or she has to get the agreement of the people or their elected representatives first.

Think about your situation at school. Is your school based more on ranking or linking? For instance, do you feel that you are linked to your teachers, because you are both working for a good education? Or are you ranked? (Maybe there's a bit of both systems working!) Think of how else people rank or link.

Living the Feudal Way

Kids of the Middle Ages were told that God owned all the land, but that God allowed certain powerful nobles to control it for Him. Some land was reserved for the Church and monasteries, where monks lived.

Kings and nobles ruled like mini-gods. On the positive side, they were supposed to protect and care for the common people. On the negative side, they could be bossy, cruel, and too quick to fight.

The feudal system created so many problems that, over the years, the word "feud" has come to mean fighting!

Chess: Medieval Game of War

Chess started in China, but became popular in Europe when people renamed the pieces as figures in their lives. In chess, two extremes, Black and White, take on the roles of Challengers and Defenders. Their goal is to defeat the enemy king and take over the board. Chess was very close to real medieval life!

Like a medieval village, the chessboard contains the following characters.

Meet the Players

A King: He's dignified and deliberate, taking only one step at a time.

A Queen: She has the power to move in any direction — up, back, across, and on a diagonal. But her move has to be a straight line.

Two Castles (also called Rooks): They move across, back and forth, protecting the king in times of danger. Kings can change places with them for greater protection, just as real kings holed up in their castles.

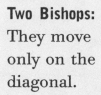

Two Bishops: They move only on the diagonal.

Two Knights: Riding on horseback they make an L-shape move, two steps forward, and one to the side.

Eight Pawns: These humble foot soldiers pay the price of war. They move one step forward at a time, attacking on the diagonal. As in real life, they're the first to fall in battle.

Setup and Playing

The board has 64 black and white squares. White has the first move; then, off you go, square by square, moving across the field of battle. Good luck capturing the other side's king!

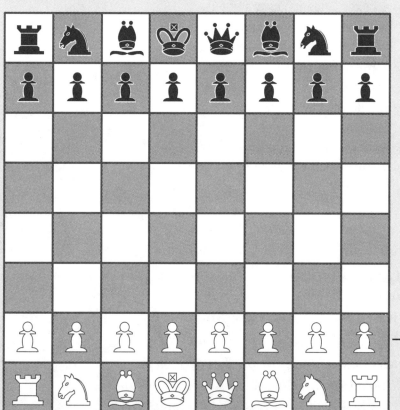

Black

— Pawns

White

Rook   Knight   Bishop   Queen   King   Bishop   Knight   Rook

THE FOUR ALLS: CREATING THE MEDIEVAL WORLD

In the days of knights and castles, the world was divided into four parts called Four Alls. These roles were said to be "fixed by God."

There were:

"the peasants who worked for all, priests who prayed for all, knights who fought for all, and kings who ruled all."

Create the Four Alls

 YOU WILL NEED:

- ✤ 4 boxes (shoe boxes are good)
- ✤ Art materials: paint and paintbrush, glue, fabric scraps
- ✤ Natural materials: grass, sticks, pebbles
- ✤ Air-drying clay (optional)
- ✤ Books, magazines with pictures of the Middle Ages (optional)

To set the scene of long ago, create a set of Four Alls dioramas, each depicting the people of the Middle Ages in their usual environments. Work alone or in a group. When the Four Alls are finished, display them (perhaps one on top of the other) as a model of medieval society.

You'll need time to work on all four, but in the end, your creation will show the basic structure of Middle Ages' society. That's impressive!

Recipe for Hard Clay

Combine equal amounts of cornstarch, white flour, and water in a saucepan. Ask a grown-up to heat the mixture while you stir over a low flame. Scoop it into a ball with a spoon, and let it cool.

Once the dough cools, push and pull it on a floured surface until it's smooth. Then, make your shapes.

To dry, leave the clay alone for two days. Or, ask a grown-up to dry in an oven set at LOW for an hour or two. Decorate with markers or tempera paint.

Let your creativity guide you as you create each world. What ideas will you come up with to bring the Four Alls to life?

To get you started, here are some ideas for the outside of your diorama:

How about painting the outside of a box sky blue and white to represent the heaven all four groups believed in? Add clouds, comets, sun, stars, rainbows, the moon, even angels, if you like.

Or, the outside can show the forest-green world of the wild woods that surrounded medieval villages and farms.

Here are some ideas for the inside:

Paint the inside of the boxes before you create the scene. White for the Church? Purple or red for the king? A landscape for the peasants? Blue for knights? You decide.

Make people out of air- or oven-drying clay, or by gluing pictures onto cardboard, cutting out the shapes, and attaching L-shaped cardboard "stands" to the backs.

A Four Alls Peasant Scene
"...the peasants who work for all"

Pity the peasants, working their lives away, with little to show for it. And yet, because of their work, the nobles lived royally! Still, peasants had their pleasures, too. There were festivals, merrymaking, and all sorts of holidays to celebrate.

Your Four Alls peasant world can be a simple farm or field scene, with growing grain, serfs, and animals working. "Hovels," the little earthen shacks peasants lived in, can be made from egg cartons turned upside down, with cutout openings as doors. Or, make hovels from clay, sticks, or mud.

Glue cut grass (fresh or dried) or lentil beans to the floor of the diorama. A pile of dry grass makes a good haystack. Build a cart with cardboard. How about adding some cutout sheep? A lump of cotton, soaked in strong tea and dried, makes good "wool."

A Four Alls Knight World
"...the knights who fight for all"

An old knight play set is great for this Four Alls knights' diorama. If you have an old cowboy set, dress the horses with ribbon and colored paper to make them into "steeds," the horses knights rode on. (Old cowboys can be converted to knights with tinfoil armor, too.)

The knights in your diorama can be charging in battle, feasting at a table, or in a tournament. Maybe you will show them at a knighting ceremony. If you have a lady in your scene, she can wear a cone hat of rolled paper with a tiny bit of tissue on top.

"Why are the Middle Ages sometimes called the Dark Ages?"
"Because there were so many knights!"

A Four Alls Church World
"…the priests who pray for all"

For your Four Alls church scene, create a cathedral or a monastery. For stained-glass cathedral windows, cut out long, narrow windows that arch gracefully on top. Cover with see-through material, like on a pasta box, or colored plastic wrap.

To make a raised cathedral roof, cut the shoe box in the middle of the top, and across the back. Lift at the center, and attach a folded piece of cardboard to make a peak.

Your cathedral can have pews and a raised altar. A thick ribbon makes a good altar cloth, and a Lego™ goblet (cup) is the perfect size for the priest's chalice (holy cup). Figures of peasants in the back and knights up front will add to the scene.

(Or how about a scene of monks in a monastary, writing books, or tending grape vines?)

A Four Alls Royal World
"…and kings who ruled all"

Your king or queen can sit on a throne made from folded cardboard or balsa wood. Carve designs with black ball-point pen.

The floor can be checkerboard squares in black and white, a typical Middle Ages' design. A narrow strip of red felt makes a royal runner to the throne.

If you like, draw a picture of a dog to lie at the Lord's or Lady's feet. Dogs were good friends then, just as they are now, and they often sat at the foot of the throne. Or add a pet squirrel for the queen!

Glue a piece of fabric to the walls of your royal "chamber" (room), as a tapestry. Cold, windy castles needed tapestries for warmth as well as beauty. (One famous tapestry shows a unicorn standing in flowers. How about drawing a unicorn on a piece of white cloth for your diorama?)

Put Them All Together: *A Medieval World Wall Hanging*

Put the worlds together as a Four Alls medieval wall hanging or decoration. Clip, staple, or string the dioramas together. Set them against the wall or hang them as a representation of the medieval world, constructed by you!

A Kid in Castle Times

Well, traveler, would you rather be a noble child or a peasant child?
Think it over before you choose!

THE LIFE OF A NOBLE KID

Ah, to be rich, a future "Sir" or "Your Highness!" You'd get to live in a castle and eat the best food. You'd have a horse of your own, plus a stable master to take care of it! You'd have servants to treat you royally.

But before you go dashing back in time to play the role of a noble child, think about this — especially if you're a boy:

Noble boys had to leave home at the age of seven! They were sent away to be raised by their parents' friends, because medieval nobles didn't want to spoil their children — especially their sons — with too much love. Noble parents thought too much kindness and tenderness would not help prepare boys for the harsh realities of life.

Also, as a noble child, you'd go to a school where teachers could punish you however they wanted to.

Maybe you'd rather be a peasant child.

THE LIFE OF A PEASANT KID

If you remember being little and happy, then you know in your heart that fun doesn't depend on what you own or where you live. A simple shack, a flowery field, or being outside while parents work the land — are all fun to kids — no matter when in history they lived!

And peasant children had no school at all to interfere with their fun. Spring was for hunting eggs and picking flowers. Summer was for swimming and fishing in the moat. In wintertime, you could tie cows' shinbones to your feet and skate across the moat!

But, food was scarce, winters were long, and luxuries and conveniences were nonexistent. Worst of all, a short life of hard labor was all that lay ahead.

Together At Play

Until about the age of seven, noble and peasant kids played together. But after seven, they took their separate — and opposite — places in life.

Kids of the Middle Ages played Hide and Seek and Blind Man's Bluff. Some juggled and walked on balance beams! If a noble kid was around, there'd be marbles to shoot, or Bocci to play (see page 70).

On holidays, peasant children were sometimes invited into the castle to play Hunt the Slipper (see page 32) or Musical Chairs.

A FLIP OF THE COIN

In a typical Middle Ages flip of the coin, the harsh life of the noble child would probably improve when the young noble grew up. The carefree life of a peasant child, on the other hand, would take a turn for the worse.

Now which do you think you'd rather be, noble or peasant child?

Play Hunt the Slipper

THE SECRET SOCIETY OF KIDS

There are games that all kids seem to know — like Hide and Seek — that have been played as long as anyone remembers. It's as if every child in every time is part of a secret society devoted to fun. Kids have a way of picking up and passing on rhymes and games that aren't found in any book.

Think about the games and rhymes you learned when you were little. Did you sing Here We Go Round the Mulberry Bush? That is an ancient oldie passed down from kid to kid, all the way from the Middle Ages to you! (See page 71.)

aFor this castle game, you need a circle of kids and a slipper or shoe. One kid, the Slipper Soul, stands in the middle holding the slipper, as the others busily pretend to be cobblers, sewing and hammering shoes.

Slipper Soul hands the shoe to one of the cobblers; then, she closes her eyes and chants:

Cobbler! Cobbler!
Mend my shoe!
Fix it up and make it new!
One, two, three, four stitches will do!

As Slipper Soul chants, the cobblers pass the shoe around their backs, trying to hide it. (If you're on the floor, pass it under your knees.)

When the chant ends, the cobblers hum and pretend to tap and sew as Slipper Soul guesses who has the slipper. If correct, that cobbler becomes the next Slipper Soul. If incorrect, Slipper Soul has to try again!

Then & Now

Growing Up Fast

In the days of knights, people were in a hurry to grow up. Boys could marry at fourteen, and girls at twelve. The reason was that only half the people lived to the age of thirty.

Now, most people live into their seventies and beyond. You will have 18 or 21 years to become an adult legally.

Do you think medieval kids missed anything by growing up so fast? At what age do you think people should be considered grown-ups? Do you like having time to be a kid?

Is Yours a Medieval Name?

At the beginning of medieval times, people had first names only. If your name was Gunther, Johann, Carlos, Kay, or Elaine, chances are you'd be the only one with that name in the village. Soon, common names expanded for clearer identification. People became, John Will's son, or Brenda redhead.

As society grew, last names were created, often from the work one did, or from the place where one was born, or a father's first name.

Many names today have their roots in those first Middle Ages' labels. How many of these names can you match to people today?

Bailey: in charge of the inner castle courtyard

Baker: mm, mmm, good

Boon: a free day of labor done as a favor for the lord, a special favor

Butler: the one in charge of bottles

Carter, Cartwright: made and fixed carts

Carver: carved meat at castle feasts

Clayton: from the Clay Town where pottery is made

Conner: an ale tester who had to sit in a puddle of ale in leather pants for hours. If his pants got sticky, the ale was too sweet!

Cooper: a barrel maker

Mason: a stone worker

Miller: an important man! He turned grain into flour for bread

Reeve: the chief peasant who reported to the lord

Smith: made tools and goods from metal

Taylor: sewed coats and garments

Thatcher: made thatch roofs

Wagner: made and fixed wagons

Ward: like bailey, named for inner section of the castle

Warner: In castle times, this pastry maker had to "warn" people in the hallways that dessert was about to be served!

Wheeler: You can probably figure this one out yourself!

The Nobles Who Rule All

magine being the most powerful lord or lady in the area — a king or queen! You'd live in a one-of-a-kind castle, designed to show your power and to protect you in times of trouble. Your castle would contain an entire city filled with people who looked to you for guidance!

Some Medieval Coins

Thalers

Pounds

Crowns

CROWN YOURSELF KING OR QUEEN

If your ancestors came from Europe, chances are you descended from peasants, because most people were peasants back then. Still, that doesn't stop you from crowning yourself king or queen today!

What would your life be like as a royal highness? Find out! Make yourself a crown, create your own currency (money) with your picture on it, too! You'd better get a good economy going to make your kingdom a success. (An economy is based on making, buying, and selling goods and services, and the earnings from those activities).

In the Middle Ages, the economy was based on sheep (for meat and wool), fighting (because swords, shields, armor, and horses cost lots of money), and farming. What would you base your economy on if you were king or queen?

Farthings

Ducats

Francs

Then & Now
Making a Profit

A profit is the gain you make in business. For instance, if an apple costs 25 cents to grow, and you sell it for 50 cents, you make a profit of 25 cents.

In our time, making a profit is the most important part of business, sometimes called "the bottom line." Without profits, there's no business.

In the Middle Ages, profits were thought to be unfair and evil! The Christian ideal was for everybody to make do and freely share what they had with others. Working after dark was considered a crime, because people working longer made more profits. How different from our views today!

In our time, a bargain is an item that we buy at a good price. Back then a bargain was a law designed to *bar* (prevent) the seller from making any *gain*, or profit!

Take on Royal Bearing

Being royal starts with the way we carry ourselves. Royalty, from the Egyptians on, has always had a certain posture, relaxed but dignified. The royal way to use your body is to let your head float upward, making you tall as you can be. Slouching is definitely for scoundrels and knaves, not for people of royal bearing.

True royals are relaxed, too. Being rich is definitely good for the posture!

LADIES OF THE COURT

Kings had queens, lords had ladies, dukes had duchesses, and barons were married to baronesses. These privileged ladies lived far better than the simple folk who served them. Ladies had straw beds raised off the ground and incredible luxuries, like soap, spices, and fine clothes. Though they were not allowed to go to school, many ladies learned to sing and play music. Girls who could sing were thought to make superior wives!

What a Mess! A Royal Feast

Questions Questions

Now that you're a king or queen, with a crown and some currency to create an economy, what will you do with all that power, Your Highness? Hmmm? Will you be a kind and gentle leader? Or a bossy bully? What will be your first proclamation shouted by the herald?

Thou loves to ribbit

Stop That Croaking!

Attending to the Middle Ages' rich would be very demanding. Peasants complained when one highborn lady ordered them to stop the frogs from croaking at night!

If you like to eat (and who doesn't?) make a medieval feast for yourself and your friends as you play the part of noble.

The medieval menu contained decorated bread, delightful salads, roasted meats, and sublime desserts called "subtleties." Between each course, there was juggling, singing, dancing, or even a play. While the servants worked, nobles and their guests enjoyed a feast of food and entertainment. And when else but in the Middle Ages could you eat salad with your fingers?

ON THE MENU: THE ROYAL CHICKEN, BEEF, OR LAMB

Vegetarians were few and far between in the Middle Ages. Nobles ate meat every day, and peasants ate whatever they could grow or catch. Herbs and spices preserved — and disguised — the taste of old meat in this time without refrigeration.

Meat was roasted, swabbed with oil. Sometimes chickens were even re-feathered for a party! Side dishes of beans and vegetables served in covered dishes and salads with many types of greens made meals complete.

Dinner was served artfully, with garnishes, small sprigs of plants to make the plates look nice. The practice of garnishing plates came from the Romans and is still around today as that parsley on your plate will attest!

Poof, Begone!
What Not to Serve

Here's what you wouldn't find on the menu of a medieval feast: potatoes, tomatoes, or anything with vanilla, chocolate, or strawberries. Those yummy foods were all introduced by the natives of North and South America, who had not yet been "discovered."

Poof, begone to cinnamon, ginger, tapioca, pepper, coriander, and curry, too. Those spices came from faraway places and were still unknown to most people.

Guess I'll have the bread and water again.

MAKE A MEDIEVAL MESS

In the Middle Ages, a "mess" was the bread under the trencher that kept the meat juices from running on the table. At the end of a feast, the mess was left uneaten. That's how we get the expression, "Clean up that mess!"

Picture This!

The Easiest Job—Setting the Table

If you lived in the year 1000, this was the job to get! There were no forks on a medieval table, just a spoon or two. And forget plates, really. Only the noblest of nobles had them. The rest of the people ate from trenchers, which were dishes made from bread.

As for the tablecloth, medieval people hung it behind them on the wall to keep the cold drafts out. Setting the table was a breeze!

Think About It:

People behaved rather crudely (to say the least!) at the dinner table in the Middle Ages. So, how did we get from spitting across the table then, all the way to chewing with our mouths closed now? Why do you think good manners evolved?

Too Rude!
Medieval Table Manners

Nowadays, good manners can be complicated. Not only are we supposed to keep our elbows off the table, but we have to know which fork or spoon to eat with, where to put the salad dish, and when to use a butter knife. But in medieval times, good manners were a cinch! Just follow these basic rules:

- ✤ **No spitting across the table.**
- ✤ **No dipping meat in the salt dish.**
- ✤ **Do not pick your teeth with a knife or finger.**

There were other rules about which fingers to use for dipping into sauces. Today's custom of holding a pinkie out while drinking from a stemmed goblet comes from the Middle Ages, when the pinkie was reserved for dipping into dessert!

Then & Now
How Upper Crust

Today, we say "upper crust," referring to wealthy or socially important people. That expression started in medieval times, when the first course in a feast was an artfully decorated loaf of bread. The pantler (person serving the bread) would slice off the artistic upper crust and serve it to the most important noble at the "high" table, or "dais" (DAY-is).

Upper crusts were decorated with rose petals, violets, herbs, and spices "painted" onto the bread before baking.

A Delight! Rose Petal Bread

This delicately flavored medieval bread is truly fit for a king or queen!

To begin, make the rose water by simmering rose petals in a small amount of water. Then, remove the petals.

In a large bowl, dissolve the yeast in the rose water. Stir sugar, salt, and some flour into the yeast. With clean hands, knead (push and pull) the dough. Add more and more flour until it won't take anymore.

Push the dough around on a floured board. When the dough becomes smooth and elastic, cover the bowl with a clean cloth, and go play for an hour!

When you return, the dough will be bigger. Punch down the dough, and divide it in half.

Form each half into a circle, oval, heart, or long loaf. Place the loaves on separate buttered baking sheets that are sprinkled with cornmeal.

Next comes the art part.

YOU WILL NEED:

For two loaves
- ✤ 1 package active dry yeast
- ✤ 1 1/2 cups (375 ml) lukewarm rose water
- ✤ 1 tablespoon (15 ml) sugar
- ✤ 2 teaspoons (10 ml) salt
- ✤ 3-4 cups (750 ml - 1L) flour
- ✤ Cornmeal and butter
- ✤ Food dye
- ✤ 1 egg white

Activity continued>

Mix a food color with a little bit of egg white to make "paint." Paint vines, leaves, flowers, snakes, or any other art on the top of the loaves.

Bake in a preheated oven for 40 minutes at 400°F (200°C).

Delicious!

Surely You Jest!

Comedy has always been used to relieve the stresses of life — and the Middle Ages was no different. Every king had a jester, or fool, whose job was to keep the people of the court laughing. Wearing a motley hat and carrying a scepter with bells, the jester told jokes to amuse the king and queen.

Be a jester, making jokes of your own. Or, if you and a friend like comedy, try a two-person king or queen and jester act. The court also had jugglers and acrobats who entertained while people ate, so if jokes aren't your thing, perhaps you would prefer to juggle some oranges or some tennis balls.

Make Up a Ballad

How about making up words and a tune for a ballad based on a story you know? Or, ask a bunch of kids to join in making up a ballad about something happening at school or a current event.

Begin by writing a rhymed poem, because medieval songs always had a fixed form. Then make up a tune to go along. (For inspiration, listen to some old Celtic music. That's about as close as we come today to medieval music.) Here's what we came up with:

The noblest queen in the land of Doggie
Is our terrier queen, Spanky.
Her tail doth wag, and we obey
For Her Majesty's saying it's time to play.
We throw her stick and she doth fetch it,
We throw her ball and she doth cetch it.
Then she rolls over and we do pet her —
She's our terrier queen
And we'll never forget her!

Troubadours

Add music to your feast! During medieval times, troubadours (TROO-bah-dors) traveled from town to town, "singing for their supper." A talented troubadour could feast with a king and charm the royal guests. His songs were often ballads — songs about love, or the glory of kings.

Strumming on a lute or guitar, a troubadour would touch people's hearts or just be a musical gossip columnist!

SPEAKING OF DOGS...

Dogs were good friends to people then, as they are now, and they often sat at the feet of kings and ate scraps from under the dining table. Squirrels were also popular pets for ladies, following an old Roman custom. As for falcons, nobles trained them as their hunting partners!

Castles: A Complete Community

Visit a Castle — Online!

Unless you travel to Europe, it's impossible to visit real medieval castles. Luckily, you can check them out on the Internet. Here are a few web sites where you can "visit" some wondrous castles!

http://www.castlewales.com

http://fox.nstn.ca/~tmonk/castle/castle

A COMPLETE COMMUNITY

The ruling noble lived with his family in the "keep" of the castle. Soldiers and weapons were "kept" there, too, as the main function of the castle was to protect the noble.

Every castle had a church, too. It was usually near the keep. That way, the noble and his family could worship conveniently.

Each lord depended on the work of the common people, so space was provided for commoners to do their work. There was a cookhouse, a separate building near the keep, where cooking was done, and craft shops for building and making things. Skilled workers lived in the back of the shops with their families.

Inside the walls was a bailey, a kind of courtyard where pens of animals were tended. Outside the castle walls were peasant hovels, fields or crops, and fairgrounds which were open meadows for festivals and tournaments.

Let's Get Gory

Well, we don't want to really, but if we're exploring the Middle Ages, there's no way around it! Castles also had murder holes, crenellations, portcullises, and dungeons. Not pleasant — but true, nonetheless.

Murder holes were holes in the wall where the people inside could dump boiling liquid onto their enemies' heads! They had crenellations (breaks in the top walls) from which arrows could be fired.

A portcullis was a heavy metal gate to shut out invaders. And if someone happened to be in the way when the huge gate came down — too bad!

Down in the cellar of the castle keep was the dungeon, where the noble kept (and punished) his enemies!

As you design and build your own medieval castle, notice how much of it is concerned with keeping people out and keeping other people in. Talk about medieval opposites! No wonder new ideas didn't develop. The fighting frame of mind doesn't encourage the sharing of ideas.

Picture This!

SIEGE!

During a castle siege (SEEJ), challengers would try to batter their way in, by ramming the main gates with huge logs! Don't feel too sorry for the defenders, though. They were busy tossing boiling oil onto their enemies' heads!

Create a Castle

YOU WILL NEED:

✤ **Large shoe box, or cardboard lid that comes on the bottom of food cans**

✤ **Small boxes (pastina size), spaghetti boxes, small round box for a round keep, egg cartons**

✤ **Toothpicks, linguini, small bamboo skewers, or Popsicle sticks**

✤ **Art materials (glue, scissors, paint, markers)**

✤ **Aluminum foil for flags (appearing to fly in the wind)**

Make it from cardboard, wood, or spaghetti. Make it from large cartons, or create a tabletop version in a cardboard lid. Whatever materials you choose, remember that your castle, like real ones of old, will be one-of-a-kind.

You may need a grown-up's help in cutting cardboard, but make sure you design your own castle. It's a good idea to make a sketch of your castle first. In fact, some kids would rather draw their castle in great detail instead of building it. That's fine, too. Or, you might do a detailed drawing and then build one. When it's finished, it will represent the real thing designed and built by you!

Walls, Drawbridge, Moat, Gatehouse, and Keep

These features were designed for the noble's safety:

The keep of a castle is a tower, sometimes round, with many stories. There, nobles slept, ate, and planned. Soldiers lived on lower stories with the dungeon below.

The gatehouse was a building behind the drawbridge where people could explain why they wanted to come in or go out.

Two walls ran around each castle complex, the inner higher than the outer.

Castles were originally built with square corners, but after being damaged easily during battles, workers began building them with rounded corners instead.

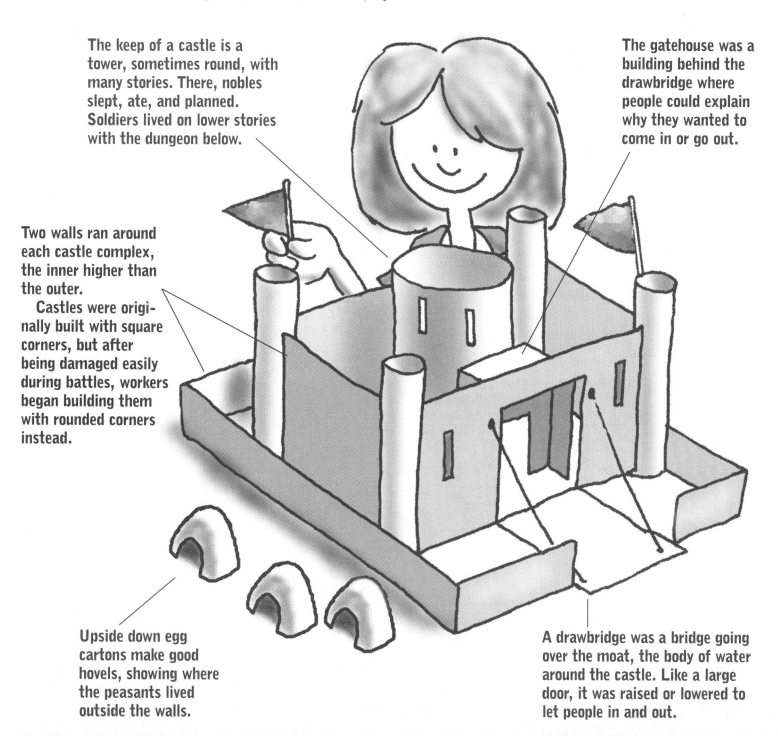

Upside down egg cartons make good hovels, showing where the peasants lived outside the walls.

A drawbridge was a bridge going over the moat, the body of water around the castle. Like a large door, it was raised or lowered to let people in and out.

Castle Building How-To

Portcullis/drawbridge pulley

Construct a pulley from a thread spool and pencil, to open and close the portcullis and/or drawbridge. Attach the pulley inside the castle wall, on top. (You may have to add cardboard to the wall.) Attach one end of string to the spool and the other to the portcullis. When you turn the pencil, the gate will raise and lower. (Use the same idea for drawbridge.)

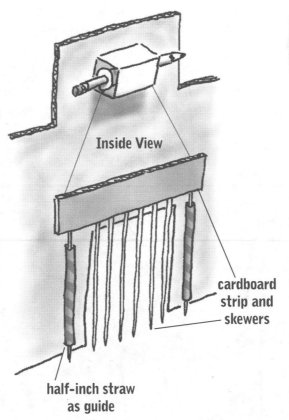

Inside View

cardboard strip and skewers

half-inch straw as guide

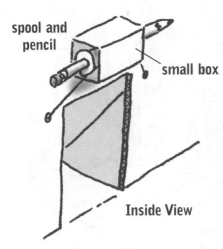

spool and pencil

small box

Inside View

Or, raise and lower the portcullis by pulling from above, as if you were a giant. To work the drawbridge without a pulley, cut a hole in the opposite wall of the castle (in back) and pull the string through.

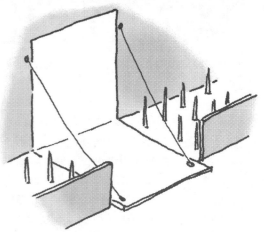

Moat with drawbridge

Paint a moat to surround the castle. Or glue pointed toothpicks in your moat, as some castle moats contained sticks instead of water.

Keep

For a castle keep, keep your eyes open for a round container, box, or can (like breadcrumb or oatmeal containers). Cover with paper and decorate.

OATMEAL

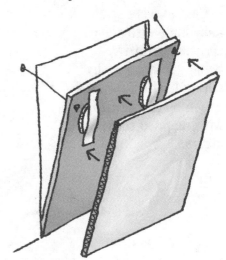

Drawbridge

Tape coins to the bottom side of the drawbridge for better opening and closing (two quarters work well). Hide the weights by gluing a piece of cardboard onto the drawbridge.

Make a Catapult

A catapult is a mechanical device that hurls objects into the air, over castle walls. Attackers used them during castle sieges.

Design a catapult from cardboard and elastic bands.

- ✤ Cardboard bath tissue tube
- ✤ 3 pieces of cardboard:
  - 2" x 3" (5 x 7.5 cm)
  - 2" x 2" (5 x 5 cm)
  - 1 square inch (2.5 cm)
- ✤ Skewer or long toothpick
- ✤ Rubber band
- ✤ Tape

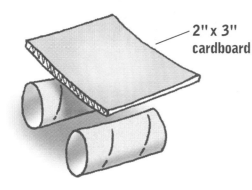

2" x 3" cardboard

1" square cardboard

2" x 2" cardboard

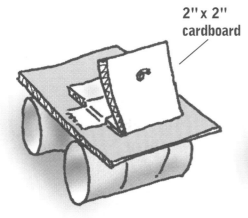

Cut the tube into wheels; then, tape the round wheels to the larger rectangle of corrugated cardboard. Fold the smaller piece of cardboard in half the short way. Now, cut the rubber band and knot one end; then, pull the band through one side of the folded board. Attach that to the body of the catapult with tape. Next, tape the stick to the upper side of the cardboard, as shown. Knot the other end of the rubber band tightly, so that only about an inch (2.5 cm) of taut band remains. Then add a 1"- (2.5 cm-) square piece of corrugated cardboard to the free end of the stick.

Try flinging dried lentils over your castle walls. How far away can you be and still hit the mark?

Fighting for All: The World of Knights

THE CALL TO BATTLE

Would you have liked the life of a knight, riding high on a horse, waving a sword of gleaming steel? To a knight, fighting was a way of life.

But the glory of battle makes for a strange lifestyle — one that is filled with those contradictory medieval opposites again. Knights spent half their lives training and fighting. The other half was spent recovering from their wounds!

"If I were stepping forward with one foot in Paradise and the other still in my castle, and someone sounded the call to battle, I would step backward again."

"I never eat, drink, or sleep so well as when I hear the war cries rise!"

PAGES AND SQUIRES: STEPS TO KNIGHTHOOD

The first step to knighthood was becoming a page. Pages were kids of 7 to 13 who delivered messages and spied for their knight.

The next step, at about the age of 14, was becoming a squire, or a knight's personal assistant. Squires polished their knight's armor (the metal outfit he wore into battle), took care of his horses, and helped him in every way.

At last, after the age of 20, if his knight approved, a squire would become a knight. From that day forward, and for the rest of his life, his title would be "Sir."

Get Dubbed

On the glorious day of your knighting, you'd kneel down on one knee in front of a powerful lord and hand him your sword, lance, and spurs. Then, cupping your hands inside his, you'd make an oath, or promise, to serve him for the rest of your life.

In response, the noble would tap you on the shoulder with the flat side of his sword and loudly declare, "I dub thee knight. Arise, Sir So and So!"

Then & Now

Sir Isaac Newton, Sir Lawrence Olivier, Sir Paul McCartney? That's right, these famous people and many others, are knights. Though the dueling duties of knights have long since disappeared into history, the tradition of knighting still lives on in Great Britain. Each year, the monarchy chooses several accomplished people, and during a ceremony at Buckingham Palace, the Queen (or King) of England "knights" each man or woman. Women who are knighted are called "Dame," instead of Sir.

Questions Questions

Do you think these words are related: page of a book, castle page, the verb "to page," and a modern electronic pager? How?

WHY DID THEY FIGHT?

The battles that raged in the Middle Ages were fought over land, power, and wealth.

Many were family feuds. When parents died, they left their land and money to only one child, the oldest son! This system made some younger brothers and sisters bitter and angry — angry enough to fight!

Wars raged when invaders attacked, too. The Vikings of northern Scandinavian lands sailed to Europe in beautiful, silent ships. They were looking to grab land for themselves. Gliding into the harbor, they'd get off their boats, raise their swords high over their heads, and run to take whatever they wanted.

Ambition, jealousy, greed, and revenge were at the root of many wars, as people fought their way up the feudal ladder, stepping on those below them and knocking down those on top. To gain power, you had to conquer.

FROM THE NORTH

Even though they caused many a bloody battle, the Vikings of Scandinavia brought some gentler values to Europe, too. They were fairer to women, for instance, and more democratic.

Over time, many Vikings settled in a part of France now called Normandy. They built some of the finest castles of Europe. One Viking descendant, William the Conqueror, changed history by invading England and claiming the British Isles in 1066!

Think About It:

The battles waged by knights for their lords were over property and power. Because of these battles, trust couldn't develop. Do you think physical fighting is a natural part of being human? What can people do to avoid physical and verbal fighting, while still standing up for themselves?

Festival of Fighting—The Tournament!

Can you imagine a battle so serious that you call it war, but so frivolous that you call it a game?

Like paintball fighting of today, tournaments — also called fracases or melees — were designed to excite! The first tournaments were wild free-for-alls. For one or two days, knights would fight with lances and spears, trying to win horses, spurs, swords, or the hand of a lady love from their competitors. Some of these events were held on a wealthy man's 21st birthday, or to celebrate a wedding.

Conflict Resolution

Poor knights! They didn't have conflict resolution skills to settle their differences. But we do!

Next time you run into a conflict, try taking these three steps to find a nonviolent solution:

1. **Without blaming anybody else, say what the problem is for you. In other words, what's wrong and what do you need in order to make it better?**

2. **Brainstorm with others for solutions. Come up with as many ideas as you can, silly or serious, to solve the conflict.**

3. **Choose the best solution and act on it right away!**

Knights would come from near and far to compete, bringing others to fight beside them, sometimes by the hundreds. Banners flying, these small armies would go after each other with wild abandon, knocking each other off horses and kidnapping prisoners, too. What a way to get the blood stirring!

Out in the woods, where the first "tourneys" took place, log "castles" were built for the ladies so they could safely watch the game. Ladies became part of the action when the opposing side kidnapped them.

Once, in a 3,000-man tournament, William of Normandy defeated ten men single-handedly, one after another. "The fracas was so great one could not have heard God thunder!" wrote King Henry III about it.

CHALLENGERS AND DEFENDERS

Every tournament had two sides, each led by a nobleman: the challengers and the defenders. The person holding the tournament had to supply the land to fight on, wooden swords, and food for the fighters. Any man from the town could participate, but he had to sign up weeks in advance.

At the end of the tournament, a big party with prizes was held. There was even dancing — for those who hadn't broken their legs, that is!

THIS HAS TO STOP!

In the High Middle Ages, the Church declared a Truce of God, saying that all kinds of fighting had to stop, at least for one or two days a week. In some places, Mondays and Wednesdays became truce days so everyone could go about their business in peace!

Finally, the Church made a law that if you played dangerous war games, you would not be allowed in church. By the end of the Middle Ages, tournaments were simply colorful pageants, with lots of flag waving and cheering.

To the Victors Go the Spoils

One of the reasons young knights liked tournaments was that they got to keep the armor, spurs, and weapons they won in the games. Armor was expensive, and fighting in a tournament was a way to get it for free.

Picture This!

Imagine doing battle with your trusty dog on your back — that's what knights did. Well, not exactly, but their suits of armor did weigh 55 pounds, about as much as your average golden retriever!

Capture the Flag

This game goes back to the days of the Middle Ages, but it's still fun to play today.

Each team gets an equal number of water balloons and its own flag. Then, both teams hide their flags (in a tree or a bush, for instance). If a player is hit with a water balloon, he or she becomes a prisoner of the other team and must be tagged by a teammate to be set free. The goal of the game is to capture all the other team's players, or get the other team's flag and carry it back to your base.

 YOU WILL NEED:

✤ **Several water balloons**
✤ **2 flags**
✤ **At least 6 players**

Did You Know?

The word tournament, or tourney, comes from the French word, *tornejer* for turning. That's because the battle often moved in a circle with knights and squires going round and round in a field, trying to get the better of each other.

Questions Questions

Do you think the tournaments were fun for the participants or do you think they ended up fighting for real?
Do you ever "pretend wrestle" with a sibling or friend? Does someone usually end up getting hurt, or is it basically a harmless way to let off steam?

QUESTS

Some knights, in legends, took on special missions, called quests. They would go off searching, for instance, for the "Holy Grail," which was the cup Jesus Christ used at the Last Supper.

To experience the thrill of a quest, make up a special task for yourself! How about searching for the earliest picture that exists of your grandparents? Or, maybe your quest will be to visit the place where you were born.

Your quest may take you different places and put you in touch with people you don't often talk to!

THE CRUSADES

The Crusades, or Holy Wars, were military campaigns in the eleventh, twelfth and thirteenth centuries, designed to win Jerusalem for the Christians. They are a good example of medieval extremes, too. During the Crusades, European soldiers and believers traveled all the way to the Middle East — mostly on foot — to wage war on anyone who wasn't Christian!

The Crusaders actually believed they were doing good by killing innocent non-Christians!

The Crusades cost Europeans a fortune in time, money, and lost lives. And, they never controlled Jerusalem for very long, either.

Then & Now

As you know, the Middle Ages was a time of great intolerance. People thought nothing of battling over differences in religious beliefs. And do you know what? Wars are still being fought over the exact same things. You can make a difference, by learning about the religions of the people on your street, in your classroom, and in other parts of the world.

Create a Coat of Arms

In the Early Middle Ages, it was hard to tell who was fighting whom during a raging battle. The knights of the twelfth century (1100s) solved that problem by creating special designs, called coats of arms, for their shields.

Some coats of arms pictured lions, feathers, dragons, eagles, falcons, crowns, diamonds, or other shapes. Often the shield was divided in half or in quarters, showing contrasting colors.

To make your shield, cut a pizzaboard into the shape of a shield or a circle. Pencil in the outline of your design first. Then fill in with poster paints. When finished, staple a corrugated cardboard handle on the back.

Make a Knight's Helmet and a Sword

A knight's helmet can be made with a rectangle of corrugated cardboard or posterboard, about 10" x 24" (25 cm x 60 cm).

Fold into a circle, like a tall crown. Attach with silver duct tape.

Cut a circle about 7 1/2" (18.75 cm) in diameter to fill in top of helmet. Tape that, too.

To make a fierce-looking helmet, cut out an M-shape in the front. Cover with aluminum foil.

For a sword, draw and then cut the shape of a handle and blade from corrugated cardboard. For extra strength, cut another of the same size and join them together with tape. Cover the sword with aluminum foil.

The Holy World of the Church
(and the Secret Life of Pagans)

During the Middle Ages, the Church was organized like a government, with laws and officers. The Church and nobles cooperated with each other to control the common people and to make sure they practiced Christianity a certain way.

But not everyone in Europe wanted to be Christian. Some people still secretly followed their traditional tribal, or pagan, beliefs. Others were wandering peoples, like Jews and Gypsies, who had their own unique beliefs.

Some ruthless lords forced these non-Christians to become Christians under pain of death! Others tried to win non-believers over with kindness. But practically no one was left alone to make up his or her own mind about what to believe.

Think About It:

In some countries, religious leaders have the authority to govern the people. In other countries — like the United States and Canada — religion (church) is kept separate from government (state). In fact, the search for religious freedom was one very important factor in the birth of the United States. What do you think are some advantages and disadvantages of each kind of government?

A LIFE IN THE CHURCH

Religion was a way to stay safe in the Middle Ages. Some young nobles probably became monks to avoid a life of endless battles.

Monks lived in large monasteries or abbeys. There, they worked and prayed, and devoted their lives to practicing religion.

During the Late Middle Ages, women formed a religious life as nuns, too. The first nun was St. Claire, a good friend of St. Francis of Assisi (see page 61).

Then & Now

Tribal People

The old tribal ways were seen as inferior by the conquering Romans and by church officials of the Middle Ages.

In many places, tribal people are still treated with disrespect. But a new way of thinking is spreading; more and more people realize that tribal ways are filled with wisdom and knowledge about nature.

Some modern scientists try to learn from native peoples. They hope to learn about healing plants from tribal healers, called Shamans.

Since tribal life does not depend on money, native people are often economically poor. Sometimes they live on land that is valuable, so others try to force them off or change their way of life.

Cultural Survival is an organization that helps native people around the world. To find out more about this modern-day struggle, contact:

Cultural Survival
96 Mount Auburn St.
Cambridge, MA 02138 USA
E-mail: csinc@cs.org
Website: http://www.cs.org

STAINED-GLASS WINDOWS

Imagine a painting made of sunlight — that's what a stained-glass window is! Light from the outside shines through the windows, illuminating a glorious picture for all inside to see.

The colored glass windows of medieval cathedrals are some of the most beautiful works of art of all time. The Rose Window of the Chartres Cathedral in France is perhaps the most famous and exquisite.

In brilliant hues, these windows vividly portray Bible stories and lives of the saints. Stained-glass windows may have been the most glorious sight most medieval people ever got to see.

To recreate the splendor of stained glass, tape colored tissue paper to a sunny window. The colors will glow brilliantly!

Take a Vow of Silence

Different kinds of monks were like teams, with special clothes (robes) and different ways of living. Some monks were teachers who taught noble children. Some worked the land of the monastery, growing herbs, or tending grapes to make wine.

Some took on the job of praying for everyone else. They believed that praying was easier if people didn't speak. These were the silent brothers, who tried to gain wisdom through silence.

How long can you stay silent? One minute? Ten minutes? Two hours? An afternoon? To find out, put a pad and pencil in your pocket and stop talking! When you need to communicate, use the pencil instead.

Illuminate a Book

Monks wrote books by hand (since printing presses had not yet been invented). Using quill pens, they wrote letter after intricate, decorative letter until an entire book was complete. They decorated the edges of the pages with beautiful, colorful pictures of vines and flowers — sometimes colored with real gold and silver. To do this, pieces of gold and silver were flattened into thin sheets and applied to the letters and pictures.

These decorations are called illuminations. (To illuminate a book of your own, see page 78.)

EASTER BUNNIES AND CHRISTMAS TREES: THE OLD PAGAN WAYS

The Church let pagans keep some of their old customs by making them part of Christianity. Also, some pagan traditions got mixed up with existing Christian holidays. That's why we have Christmas trees and Easter bunnies and eggs today!

Rabbits and eggs are ancient signs of fertility, often symbolizing the hope for abundant crops and food for all. As for Christmas trees, read on....

HEY!

Picture This!

Imagine a book trimmed in gold with letters embellished with intricate, brilliantly colored designs. That's what The Book of Kells *is like. This book was a magnificently decorated text of the Four Gospels of the New Testament. It was created during the eighth or ninth century by Irish monks.*

THE CHRISTMAS TREE— A GIFT OF THE DRUIDS

Decorating a tree in wintertime is an ancient Druid custom that became part of Christianity during the Middle Ages. (For more about Druids, see page 14.)

Druids believed that trees could teach people a lot about life. Trees have deep roots to help them to stand up against storms, they lift their leafy arms (branches) up to the heavens, and they grow straight and tall.

The Druids' holy places were groves of ancient trees. Many cathedrals of Europe, including the famous Chartres Cathedral of France, were built on these old Druid sites to literally displace the old pagan religion with the new Christian one.

EXTREMELY HOLY!

The word "holy" means whole — being all together and undivided. With all the divisions and conflict of medieval times, no wonder people wanted holiness. (One more medieval opposite in action!)

Medieval people believed that certain super-good people called saints were so holy that their spirits glowed. Artists painted light around their heads, or halos (HAY-los) — sometimes with real gold. You can paint pictures of people and add halos of gold glitter.

Druid Riddles

One of the ways that Druids passed their wisdom on was through riddles. Can you answer these ancient riddles?

✤ 1. What is sweeter than a sweet drink?
✤ 2. What is blacker than the raven?
✤ 3. What is whiter than snow?
✤ 4. What is swifter than the wind?
✤ 5. What is sharper than the sword?
✤ 6. What is lighter than a spark?

Answers: 1. A good talk with someone who loves you 2. Death 3. Truth 4. Thought 5. Understanding 6. An idea

Saint Francis of Assisi

Saint Francis of Assisi brought light to the Middle Ages because he had so much love to share. To him, every creature on the earth was important and special. He called animals his "brothers and sisters" because they, too, were made by God. He even knelt down to help the earthworms get off the road on rainy days!

Though he was born to nobles, Francis decided to live simply and help the poor. He started The Franciscan Brothers, an order of monks who are still doing good in the world today!

Think About It:

Closed Minds or Open?

An open mind is ready for new ideas. A closed mind thinks it knows everything already.

Some people close their minds because new ideas can be frightening. But how can we possibly expect to understand everything in this big process called life? The answer is, we can't! Being open-minded sometimes means not knowing and feeling uncomfortable with new ideas and new ways of doing things. Can you think of something you may be "close-minded" about? Open your mind and explore the possibilities!

St. Francis's prayer is one of the most beautiful poems of the Middle Ages. You don't have to be Christian to understand and treasure these wise thoughts.

**Lord, make me an instrument of thy peace.
... Where there is darkness, let me shine light.**

MANY WAYS TO BELIEVE

Spiritual and religious beliefs come in many different forms. How many different Christian religions can you list? How many other religions can you name? Make a list, and ask everyone you know to help. (Hint: There are more than you probably ever imagined!) When you are finished, look up "religious organizations," "church," "synagogue," or "temple" in the yellow pages of your phone book. How many are listed there?

The Rugged World of the Peasant

Snobbery in Action

The following statements were all written during the Middle Ages:

"Fish are like peasants, for a fish is ever naked and cold."

"The peasant's head is so hard that no idea can get into it."

"The Devil himself will not take peasants because of their awful smell."

"These rustics we might call a species of cattle."

Peasants! They were often treated badly, even though it was their hard work that made the days of knights and castles possible.

A democratic-minded writer of the time had this to say:

Some ploughed with the plough
Their play was but seldom
Some sowing, some earning,
With the sweat of their brows,
The gain which the great ones
In gluttony waste!

(Gluttony means eating too much.)

HOME, SWEET HOVEL

Think About It:

If you were a peasant your house would be no house at all—it would be a windowless "hovel," or earthen shack, made from sticks, mud, or even dried cow manure.

If you were lucky, there'd be a table, bench, and one chair to sit on. Your family would probably own one large bowl, a few wooden spoons, and a knife. Home, sweet hovel was as humble as can be.

Who Writes the History Books?

What we call history — the tales of kings and battles — tells us only about the lives of a small fraction of the people who lived during the Middle Ages.

History tells of quests and glory, of splendor and honor. But most people back then were workers whose lives were spent serving the nobles. These working people often went hungry so that richer people could feast.

If peasants had been able to write the history books, do you think they would have told a different story? What do you think they would have said?

Think About It:

Everyone has some good qualities — even someone you "don't like." Think about just one good quality about that person, like, "Karen has the nicest smile of anyone," or, "Jason is really smart in math class." Name one act of kindness you could do to help someone less fortunate than you feel good about himself.

SNUGGLING WITH PORKY

At night, you and your family would pile onto a "mattress"— a lump of straw on the floor. Blankets were luxury items. If it was cold, you'd have your mom and dad, and your sisters and brothers to keep you warm, since the whole family slept in the same bed.

And if your family didn't snuggle you, there was always the family pig. If she was friendly, she'd sleep in the bed, too. In early medieval times, people brought all their farm animals inside on cool nights — even cows!

PEASANT-STYLE

If you like a rustic look in a room, do what peasants did back in the Middle Ages. Hang bunches of lavender, basil, mint, and other herbs on the wall. Not only did they look nice, the herbs also provided spices and medicines in the wintertime. They kept the air smelling sweeter, too!

If you don't have a garden to grow herbs, buy a bunch at the supermarket. Bundle them with string or ribbon, and hang them upside down from a nail. The dried herbs will last for months.

Cleaning Up, Medieval-style

The Middle Ages weren't exactly a time of supreme cleanliness. In fact, they were far from it. People bathed about once a month, and peasants wore the same clothes day after day. That's because most people, except the wealthy, had only one outfit to wear.

But when cleaning time finally rolled around, medieval people used herbs instead of chemicals. They tossed lavender flowers into the water with results that were sniff, sniff, ahhhh— excellent! Mint was used for cleaning, too.

Modern scientists say that mint and lavender have chemicals in them that keep fleas away. With all the animals and straw in the house, medieval people needed all the flea repellents they could get!

"You, too?"

Lucky, Lucky

Believe it or not, you live far better than the wealthiest king or queen of the Middle Ages. Some of the everyday items that you frequently use would be incredible luxuries to medieval people. Clean, running water, a machine that lets you speak to people far away, and a cupboard that keeps food cold, even in summer, would be magic to them!

So next time you use a bar of soap, or sprinkle pepper on your food, and even flush a toilet, take a minute to appreciate how fortunate you really are.

Then & Now
Chairman

The word "chairman" comes directly from the Middle Ages, when a house had only one chair, for the exclusive use of the man of the family. In those days, "a man's home was his castle."

That belief is fine — unless you are a woman or child! (Maybe we can change it to, "a person's home is his or her castle!")

A Rose Petal Necklace

Think About It:

Some people long for less-complicated times when people worked hard but life seemed simpler. Today, we live life in the fast lane: With computers and the Internet, we can communicate in an instant; with airplanes, we can cross oceans in a matter of hours; with modern medicine, we can live to ripe old ages. Which kind of lifestyle suits you best, or do you prefer some things about both lifestyles?

Even a peasant girl could enjoy a rose petal necklace. Roses grew wild and the petals were free! Snip or pinch off the white part of the rose petals.

Roll the petals into tight little balls and thread them into a necklace. For another special rose necklace, string dried rosebuds as a necklace.

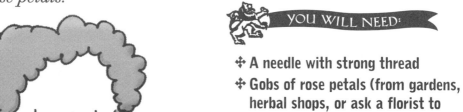

YOU WILL NEED:

❖ **A needle with strong thread**
❖ **Gobs of rose petals (from gardens, herbal shops, or ask a florist to save you roses that have gone by)**

Picture This!

Remember the knights, the lords, and the lowly peasants? Picture all three: the knight in his suit of armor atop his powerful steed; the lord dressed in fur-trimmed velvet robes, feasting at a long table; the peasant dressed in tattered clothes with cal-luses on his hands from hard work. Now, pick one and write about a typical day in his or her life. Make it fun. Get into character. Pretend you are the person you are writing about. How does the day compare with a real day in your life?

Come One, Come All! Medieval Merrymaking!

"When life is hard, celebrate!"

That seems to have been the motto of medieval times, when almost half the days of the year were some holiday or other. (Another example of medieval extremes.) Some of those holidays — like Valentine's Day, April Fools' Day, and Hallowe'en — are still part of our lives today.

ST. VALENTINE'S DAY

There are lots of stories about St. Valentine and little agreement about who he really was and where he really lived. Still, somebody named Valentine once had the brilliant idea of sending everybody he loved a note to tell them of his appreciation. The inspiration must have struck on February 14th, too. But the cards he created would be a brilliant idea any day of the year!

BELLS, BONES, AND PSALTERIES

Jingling bells and clattering bones were the simplest musical instruments. Bells were tied to the branches of trees and carried through the town on holidays. Bones clapping together made the music around many a bonfire.

If there are steak-eaters in your house, save the T-bones (clean them off, and soak them in bleach and water before using; remember bleach is poisonous, so ask an adult to supervise). Then, use them as clackers. Look for a fallen stick and string bells on it for a simple jingling shaker, too. Use these instruments for the Oranges and Lemons game (see page 70) and other musical chants you find in this book.

Fancier instruments of that time were lutes and psaltery, a stringed instrument that was used when holy songs were sung.

Sing *A Capella*

Singing a song without musical instruments accompanying you is called singing a capella— a style that harks back to the Middle Ages. Singing in this way can be challenging, but its simplicity is quite beautiful. Listen to a favorite song and try to sing it without any accompanying music. Does it help to hear the music in your head?

APRIL FOOLS' DAY

Maybe it's because society was so rigid and serious, but having a day of nonsense was vitally important to medieval people. April Fools' Day (April 1st) was set aside for sheer silliness, and often there was a Widdershins Day, too. (Or should we say, yad snih-sreddiw.) What's that? On read.

Widdershins — Snihsreddiw

Any day can be Widdershins Day, when everything is done backwards. Gnihtyreve!

To celebrate Widdershins Day, start your morning by eating supper. When your family comes into the kitchen, wish them, "Good night!"

Walk out the door backwards and walk backward to the bus stop. When you see a friend, tell her, "Bye! I had a nice time today." Then tell her about Widdershins Day. Greet everyone you see with a cheery, "Bye! See ya! Take care!"

Do your homework, last problem first. Start your "breakfast" with dessert, and

finish up with salad or soup.

When you climb into bed at night, be sure to wish your mother "Good morning."

HALLOWE'EN

Dressing in costume and roaming the neighborhood for candy is our modern way of celebrating a very ancient holiday. "All Hallows' Evening" was the Christian version of Summer's End or "Samhain," which is the Druid New Year. On this one special night, pagans would pray to the forces of darkness, asking for their protection during the coming winter.

Some believed that the souls of the dead would come and visit at the kitchen hearth on that night. So people stayed home, patiently waiting for their loved ones who had passed away to return for a visit in spirit form.

Hallowe'en costumes started with pranksters trying to trick the waiting believers into thinking their dead relatives were actually walking around outside!

Wassail a Fruit Tree

YOU WILL NEED:

✦ **A tankard — any large mug will do**
✦ **Apple cider**
✦ **Sunflower seeds**
✦ **One or more people**

Bob for Apples

This custom has been going on since the Middle Ages. That's a thousand years of fun!

Fill a large bucket (or sink) with water; then, float some apples in it. Everyone takes turns trying to get a bite of an apple without using their hands. Have towels ready!

In spring it's time to wassail — or toast — a local fruit tree by singing, stamping the ground to wake up the roots, and giving the tree food. Supposedly, wassailing would charm the tree into making lots of fruit. Wassailing is noisy magic!

You can wassail indoors or out. If indoors, use a potted tree, or one of papier-maché, as castle dwellers once did.

Start a rhythm and keep it going. Then, circle the tree, chanting:

Hail to thee, old apple tree!

From every bough

Give us apples enow ✦

Hatsful, capsful,

Bushel, bushel sacksful,

And our arms full, too!

Stop and lift your cider-filled tankards to the tree. Take a drink, and eat a seed. Then, circle again, chanting more slowly this time. After the second chanting, stop and give the tree food and drink by pouring cider at the roots and leaving seeds.

Circle and chant a third time. Make it as loud and fast as you can. Stamp your feet, hoot and shout! This is to wake up the tree roots and let them know it's spring. That's what wassailing is all about!

✦(old word for enough, pronounced ee-now)

Oranges and Lemons

This lively game was played by two teams wearing orange or yellow clothing. (A sheet of orange or yellow construction paper taped on a shirt works fine, too.)

Two players, one in orange, the other in yellow, form an arch with their arms. The other players line up and pass under the arch as the "Oranges and Lemons" song is sung or chanted.

The person passing under the arch after words "chop off your head" is now a prisoner who must choose to be on the orange or lemon team. The chant continues until everyone is on a team.

Then there is a friendly tug-of-war, with the winners being called "Spring" and the losers being called "Winter."

YOU WILL NEED:

❖ **A group of kids who want to have fun**

❖ **Orange and yellow feathers, hats, shirts, or markers**

Oranges and Lemons!
Say the bells of St. Clements
You owe me five farthings
Say the bells of St. Martins
When will you pay me?
Say the bells of old Bailey
When I grow rich
Say the bells of Shoreditch
When will that be?
Say the bells of Stepney
I do not know
Says the great bell of Bow
Here comes a candle to light
   you to bed
Here comes a chopper to
   chop off your head!

Play Bocci with Your Family

In medieval times there were no computer screens or TVs to take up a family's time. After dinner, families played games together to have fun and relax.

Bocci (BAH-chee) is a fun game for kids and grown-ups to play together. It's played outside, on a small patch of lawn. Bocci is easy but challenging, and best yet, anyone from age 4 to 104 can play! Next time the relatives visit, get out some Bocci balls and give this very old-time game a try.

YOU WILL NEED:

❖ **At least two sets of balls in different colors. Tennis balls are fine if you mark them.**

❖ **A small Bocci, like a golf ball**

The object of the game is to roll your ball closest to the Bocci. The youngest person tosses the Bocci on to the lawn and then, one by one, everyone gets two chances to roll their ball as close to it as they can get.

MAYPOLE AND MORRIS DANCES — MIDNIGHT MERRYMAKING

Joining hands and dancing in a ring — dancing with scarves flying in the air — is Morris dancing at its best! The Maypole celebration was a time of happiness and achievement.

The festivities started the night before the actual celebration, when people went into the woods at midnight, to "gather the May." They looked for flowers to make into crowns, garlands, and bouquets.

The next day there were festivities with contests to see who was fastest, loudest, smallest, strongest, and shrewdest. Colorful ribbons were tied to the top of a long pole or tree, and when the dancing began, the tree was tied up in ribbon finery.

All sang:
Here we go round the merry Maypole
The merry Maypole, the merry Maypole
On a cool and happy May morning!

Make up a new melody for the new season or use the "Mulberry Bush" tune. Add these verses and actions for more fun:

"This is the way we gather the May" (pretend to pick flowers and pull vines to make wreaths)

"This is the way we stamp for spring" (stamp, hoot, and wassail the tree roots)

"This is the way we Morris dance" (Fling a scarf overhead, and turn and spin. Whooping is definitely allowed!)

Midsummer's Eve

June 21st — Midsummer's Eve — is the longest day of the year. This night was an ancient holiday — a night of mystery and magic.

Join in a circle, holding hands, and chant the traditional medieval chant for Midsummer's Eve:

Green is gold
Fire is wet
Fortune's told
Dragon's met

SECRET MEANING OF THE CHANT

At Midsummer, the sunlight and moonglow make green trees look golden. So "green is gold."

People used to set candles, floating across the moat, each standing for a wish. If the candle made it across while still lit, your wish would come true. So, "fire is wet and fortune's told."

As for "dragon's met," the traditional story of "St. George and the Dragon" was performed every Midsummer's Eve. Read on....

Enter the Players!

Blast the trumpets! Jingle the bells! When the players arrive, entertainment begins! Back in the days before movies and TV, performances were "all the way live," done by wandering troupes of actors or by mummers (people in the community who liked to disguise themselves and act).

But folks in the Middle Ages weren't the only ones with talent! Get a few friends together and put on your own performance of "St. George and the Dragon." This action-packed version is made of 95 percent old lines and a few modern ones we threw in just for fun.

YOU WILL NEED:

- ✤ A large room, and one or two rehearsals
- ✤ 2 crowns, and a horn to announce the play
- ✤ Sword, helmet, and shield (page 55)
- ✤ Princess's cone hat (optional)
- ✤ A dragon costume — any crazy concoction will do! (The dragon can even have two heads if you have an extra actor and a bathrobe large enough to hide the two bodies.)
- ✤ A frying pan, the older the better
- ✤ An audience, of course!

St. George and The Dragon

A SHORT DRAMATIC COMEDY WITH TWO EXCELLENT FIGHT SCENES

CAST OF CHARACTERS:

A Herald
A Fierce Dragon
A Kindly King
A Petite Princess
St. George
An Old Doctor

Herald: *(to audience)*

Good gentles, you are here today
To see our humble play:
"St. George and the Dragon."
Enter now, the dragon!

{The Dragon enters.}

Dragon:

I am the dragon, here are my jaws!
I am the dragon, here are my claws!
I seek meat! Meat! Meat!
Meat for me to eat!

Herald:

Enter, the king and princess

King: *(to the audience or Princess)*

He says he'll rip the land apart,
If we do not feed him.
This dragon has no heart,
And we cannot flee him.

Princess:

> Then feed him, Papa.

Dragon:

> Yes! I am hungry! I am wild
> I must now — eat a child!
> Well, hello, there, Miss.

King:

> Woe is me, darling daughter.
> To be alive to see your slaughter.

Princess:

> Fear not, Good King,
> My life I give to save the land.
> On heaven's ground
> I soon shall stand.

Herald:

> Enter St. George

> *{George is riding on his steed. He sees her.}*

George:

> By God, a beautiful damsel in
> distress is she!
> Good day, lady.

Princess:

> Good youth, spur on your horse
> Fly away! Take another course!
> This dragon is about to grind me
> in his dreadful jaws!

George:

> I will not take one step from here
> Unless I rescue you from fear.
> My horse, my sword, my shield and I
> Will bring this monster forth to die!

> *{Now comes the first fight scene (see page 74), with lots of growling and drama. The dragon and George struggle until George appears to win. The dragon grovels at his feet, whimpering.}*

George: *(to princess)*

> Now place your belt around his neck,
> Tame as a dog, he will not hurt a speck.

> *{They all begin to walk away slowly, but the belt slips off the dragon's neck. The second big fight scene begins. The dragon attacks the princess by pulling her hair. He wounds George and the king, too. But George manages to stab him. At this point, everyone, including the dragon, is in bad shape. Into this walks the old doctor.}*

Herald:

> Enter the old doctor.

Old Doctor:

> I am the Doctor — I cure all ills.
> Just gulp my potions and swallow my pills.
> I can cure the itch, the stitch,
> The pox, the palsy, and the gout.
> All pains within, and all pains without.

> *{He hands pills to all.}*

> Get up, Good King! Get up, his daughter!
> You are too good to end in slaughter.

> *{The doctor moves to St. George.}*

> Get up, St. George, old England's knight.
> You wounded the dragon, I'll finish the fight.

> *{George pops up. The doctor forces a pill down the weakened dragon's throat. With sound and fury, the dragon threatens, thrashes, thuds, and dies.}*

Herald:

> So ends our tale, with a round of applause.
> Now you can give to a very fine cause.

> *{Holds out a frying pan to the audience.}*

> For in my hand is a frying pan,
> We're here to collect all the money we can!

> *{All performers collect donations from the audience.}*

The End

Ye Olde Stage Fighting

To dazzle your audience during the fight scenes, practice some action-packed stage fighting. Follow the directions skillfully and no one gets hurt. These moves are an optical illusion in action and will trick any audience.

Steps to Stage Punches

Both players look at each other and silently count to three.

1. The puncher's fist is raised to shoulder level.
2. The fist is pulled back.
3. The fist and the punchee's face move in the same direction as a real punch would take them.

The fist misses the face by a mile, of course, but it doesn't look that way to people in the front. Practice saying the numbers out loud at first.

The skill of the stage punch is the acting. On the count of one the punchee begins to look frightened. On the count of two, she looks terrified. On the count of three, she swings her face, pretending to be hurt.

Adding the Sound

Experiment to find the best slap sound. Another actor can do it, or the puncher can slap his other hand against his hip, making the sound.

Hair pulling

This illusion is truly alarming! The audience will be sure that someone is getting her hair pulled out by the roots! And it doesn't hurt one little bit with skillful stage fighting, because no hair is grabbed.

The actors stand facing each other. The puller then says something threatening like, "Why you little!" Next, the puller makes a fist and simply places it on top of the pullee's hair. (Some actors pretend there's a powerful magnet holding it on.)

The pullee then reaches up and wraps her hands around the puller's wrist. She holds the fist onto her own head. To the audience, it looks exactly as if hair is being pulled!

Once again, the secret is in the acting. The puller must appear angry and mean. The pullee must act upset, as if her hair was actually being pulled.

The Light of Learning

Imagine if all books were kept in places where no one could go to read them. In the Middle Ages, old Greek, Roman, and Jewish books and Bibles were housed in monasteries. Church officials thought that reading them would confuse people, or the books would be damaged in battles.

But though the light of learning was dim in the Middle Ages, it never went out entirely — as you'll soon see.

INFORMATION

Maybe the worst part about the Middle Ages was that practically everybody thought they knew everything back then. Duh, and double duh!

Many medieval workers were perfectly sure that

- ❖ The earth was flat
- ❖ Eating basil hatched snakes in your head
- ❖ Eating eggs caused freckles
- ❖ Noble people and peasants had different blood

- ❖ Dragons roamed the edges of the oceans
- ❖ A person would burn in hell forever if he or she ate meat on certain days
- ❖ Fireflies were the souls of babies who died before being christened

School Daze

Students were beaten with willow branches, or punched and kicked if they didn't know their lessons or disrupted the class. Luckily, discipline is much more civilized today!

How is discipline handled in your classroom? How would you handle students who interrupt the class?

Latin Spoken Here

The Middle Ages was a bilingual time, with two languages spoken in every town. One language was Latin, spoken by a few church officials and by educated people. The other was the local language, spoken by everyone else.

The Romans had tried to make Latin the only language, but it never caught on. During medieval times, Latin "died" as a spoken language.

It lived on in other ways, though. Latin got mixed into the languages of the tribes Rome had ruled. That's how Latin turned into the modern Romance languages of French, Spanish, Italian, Rumanian, and Portuguese. Latin also survived as a language of learning. Even today, the scientific names of plants are written in Latin.

Common name: *lavender*
Latin name: *Lavandula angustifolia*

Recipe for Modern English

Take 55 percent words spoken by the ancient Angles tribe. Mix in 40 percent Latin words. Sprinkle with words from Africa, Asia, Arabia, Scandinavia, Greece, and everyplace else. English is a spicy way to talk!

CAN YOU SPEAK, *SPRECH*, OR *PARLE?*

In our global world today, understanding grows when people speak more than one language. One way to get started is by saying "Good day!" in different languages.

Practice these phrases out loud, and one day they may help you make a friend!

French: *Bonjour*
Spanish: *Buenos dias*
Portuguese: *Bom dia*
Dutch: *Goeda middag*
Italian: *Buon giorno*
English: *Good day*
German: *Guten tag*

Quick! Which of those languages do you think come from Latin (Romance) roots? Which do you think come from the old German tribes (Germanic)? Hint: The Latin word for good is *bon*.

Think About It:

Making an Effort

Learning a second language certainly isn't easy, but it is well worth the effort. Why not start a French or Spanish club in your school? Instead of memorizing, learn a few words at a time and then play games, have pretend conversations, and put on a skit using part English and part your second language. It's fun and you'll be amazed at how fast you learn.

Did You Know?

The word "university" means a place where the whole universe can be studied.

Math Blues: Sound Familiar?

A twelfth-century bishop wrote: "The despair of doing sums oppressed my mind so that all my previous labor spent on learning seemed nothing. At last, by the help of God's grace and endless study, I managed to grasp ... what they call fractions."

THANK YOU, AFRICANS, JEWS, AND ARABS!

During the Middle Ages, when the people of Europe were endlessly battling and storing books away, the people of Africa kept the flame of learning burning bright. In the year 970, a great university was founded in North Africa, where students and scholars explored math, astronomy, and all forms of science.

One of the ideas that came from the university was the notion of zero. It's hard for us to imagine math without zero, but no one had ever thought of it before. The idea of zero was invented by an Arab in Africa and made popular by a Jew. Now that's cooperation!

Make a Book of Days

Rare and wonderful — that's what books were in the Middle Ages. Each was a one-of-a-kind creation, handwritten and bound in leather. (See page 59.)

Only the richest or most scholarly people possessed books in those days. A wealthy woman or man might have a "Book of Days" filled with prayers or stories of saints. In a time without calendars, the act of writing daily in a diary was a way to mark the passage of time.

A   B   C   D   E   F   G   H   I (NO: J)   K   L   M

What to Put Inside

A Book of Days (or hours, weeks, or months) makes a great gift. For a real medieval experience, how about writing with the juice of dark berries? If you find a large feather, wash it and snip the end on the diagonal for a "quill" pen. Markers or fountain pens work fine, too.

Here are some suggestions for what to put inside your Book of Days:

A week of wise sayings: *Whether you, or your grandma, or somebody famous said it, collecting pieces of wisdom is a wonderful gift. It causes you to stop and think. Ask seven people that you know and trust to provide a saying for each day.*

A book of birthdays: *In this book, you can jot down the birthdays of your family and friends so that you won't forget them. Make twelve pages, one for each month. Next to each entry, you might write down a comment about what makes that person special to you.*

A poetry book: *This book can contain short poems written by you, your friends, or other poets. This makes a perfect gift, because poems stimulate the imagination in both the writer and the reader.*

Writing Style Tips

Calligraphy (cal-LIG-graph-ee) is the art of lettering. For kids nine or older, it's a skill well worth learning. The writers in the Middle Ages used decorative lettering when writing, but your best cursive, clearest printing, or even cutting and pasting of words is fine, too.

Leave room at the edges for illuminations (see page 59). You can draw flowering vines climbing around the sides of the pages of your book.

Medieval monks colored special words or letters to make them stand out. The first letter on the page, or a saint's name, would be in red, for instance, with the rest of the writing blue or black. What will you highlight in this way?

N   O   P   Q   R   S   T   U   (NO: V)   W   X   Y   Z

Binding Your Book

The handmade books of the Middle Ages had pages made of parchment (the thin skin of young animals after it's been cleaned and dried). Parchment pages were bound together with leather. You can use cloth-covered cardboard, grocery bag paper, or even a chamois cleaning cloth (which is actually made of sheepskin) for your book.

Fold the pages and sew them with three or four large stitches.

Old-fashioned or High-tech?

Computers and electronics make books seem old-fashioned to some. But are they really? Think about books as technology. It's pretty incredible to have so many words, ideas, and images at your fingertips. And unless you have a laptop computer, you can't curl up on a sofa, or sit under a tree reading. When it comes to ease and comfort, books are hard to beat!

Write a Family History Book

Write the history of your family in the form of a history book. You can tell the story of how your parents met, for instance, and that can lead up to your birth, and the birth of your brothers and sisters, if you have any. Use old-fashioned English, which you will notice, has a comforting rhythm, or cadence.

Here's a piece of writing, told as history, about how two future parents met:

"Twas on an early morn, many years ago, when a bold, young knight named Sir Daddus rode forth on his steed. A goodly steed it was, named Toyota, bearing the color, bright blue.

"Little did Sir Daddus know that he was about to meet Lady Mom, a fair damsel with eyes of brown and hair of frosted mists. For Lady Mom was in the bank, sorting through the King's documents as was her labor. Lady Mom spied Sir Daddus at the front of the line. 'My good sir,' she said, 'Are you ready?' 'Lady, I am ready and more,' he replied, 'For I am stricken with love.'"

People who can read and write — like you! — are called literate (LIT-er-at). But can you imagine going through life without reading books? Your life would be so empty, and you would know far less than you do. Pictures on a page would stimulate your mind, but if you couldn't read, you would never learn any details. A world without reading is sad and empty.

Then & Now

The Gift of Literacy

Hardly anybody could read or write in the Middle Ages. But did you know that even today, there are many people who cannot read? These people somehow missed learning to read in school, or moved to this country having learned another language.

Some adults and children help others learn to read at school or the library. They are "literacy volunteers." Is there someone you know who needs help with reading? Perhaps you could be the teacher and change that person's life forever!

Lost, but Not Forgotten

Most music that survived medieval times is called sacred music. Since peasants couldn't read or write, most of the songs that were passed down over time were those written down by literate monks. Peasants passed on their songs and stories verbally, or by oral tradition. Sadly, much of what they knew was never put in writing.

HOW DIVINE! A WAY TO UNDERSTAND

In the Middle Ages, people believed in the magic of nature. To gain information about the world, they used their intuition, an inner way of knowing. They called this process "divination."

Divining is feeling for answers, using our senses to understand God's universe. Even today, there are talented "water diviners" who can "feel" for water under the earth. They hold a forked branch and walk on land until a feeling pulls the branch downward. That's where water will be found supposedly. We

modern people do not understand how divining works, when it works, but we know it sometimes does.

In the Middle Ages, if a plant had a speck of red, for instance, they thought it might be good for healing a cut, or to make blood strong. If flowers were bright and sunny, they thought munching them might change a sad mood.

Divining from nature may not be scientific, but it certainly is an interesting activity.

To divine, go outside to a place where there are plants and trees. Let yourself find one plant or tree to divine. Take a deep breath and close your eyes, while still facing the plant. With your eyes closed, silently ask, "What can you teach me? What is your purpose?" Make up an answer in your imagination. What secrets will you learn from the plants, flowers, and trees?

Quick Yes and No Answers

Back then people used daisies to tell if someone loved them, something people still do today, for fun. Picking off a petal at a time, the person says, "She loves me, she loves me not," and so on, till the last petal gives the answer — or not.

Another way to get an answer was counting seeds in an apple. An odd number meant "no"; an even number stood for "yes."

DOCTOR, DOCTOR!

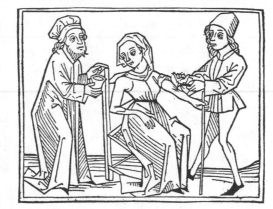

Medical science was not very advanced in the Middle Ages, when one common treatment for ailments was blood-letting, or "bleeding." The doctor cut a vein in the arm of the patient and let the blood drip out! They thought the bad "stuff" that was making the person sick would come out with the blood.

Another medical treatment was swallowing a piece of sheepskin cut like a star.

EXTREMELY OUT THERE: SCIENCE AND FANTASY

It's another case of medieval conflict: science and fantasy were all mixed up. The same brilliant mind that designed a towering cathedral could still believe that chewing the seed of a fern would make a person invisible. (Don't try it. We already did, and it definitely doesn't work.)

Serious thinkers spent endless hours arguing over how many angels could dance on the head of a pin!

Then & Now

Natural Medicine

The Saxons (and other tribes) used plants for medicine. Their "wicca" was earth wisdom, practiced by "wise women" or "wizards."

But the medieval churchmen, doctors, and nobles didn't like these ancient tribal practices. They seemed to fear the secrets the "wicca" might possess. In 1000, they proclaimed that people practicing "wicca" were from the devil. They had thousands of innocent women and some men — mostly Saxons — burned at the stake as witches!

Today, plants that the tribes used are being rediscovered by science as good medicine. Herbal remedies can be found in many health food stores and drugstores.

Grow a Medieval "Drugstore"

In the Middle Ages, parsley, sage, rosemary, and thyme were thought to be powerful protectors of good health. People put these herbs to all sorts of uses. Grow and use them today to experience what people did long ago.

Your herbs need lots of sun for good growing. Grow parsley from seeds, but sage, rosemary, and thyme do better if you fill pots halfway with potting soil and put the plants in. Fill in with more soil to cover the roots, and pat it down to fill any air pockets. Water gently a couple times a week.

To use the herbs, snip the older leaves.

YOU WILL NEED:

❖ **Four flower pots, at least 6" (15 cm), or one window box**
❖ **A sunny windowsill or spot outside**
❖ **Potting soil**
❖ **Seeds or baby plants**

Activity continued>

Parsley

When Charlemagne, king of the Holy Roman Empire, planted parsley in his "garden of good health," he knew what he was doing. Here are just a few of the nutrients in this deep-green leafy plant:

- ✤ Protein
- ✤ Iron
- ✤ Carbohydrates
- ✤ Vitamin A *(lots!)*
- ✤ Calcium *(lots!)*
- ✤ B vitamins
- ✤ Phosphorus
- ✤ Vitamin C

Thyme (pronounced Time)

Medieval people were certain that thyme gave people courage. Ladies even sewed sprigs of the plant onto scarves they made for knights going off on a quest. The patterns of leaves in many illuminations are pictures of winding thyme.

Thyme was a spice and a cough drop, too, and it still is used for that today! Look for cough drops in a health food store. A popular brand from Switzerland contains thyme.

Sage

The knights of the Crusades (see page 54) brought this silvery plant back to Europe when they returned from their quest in the Holy Land. There, Arab physicians told them that eating sage would make a person live forever! This thought pops up in the English saying, "He that would live for aye (forever) must eat sage in May!"

The French call sage, *tout bon* (pronounced TOOT-bohn), meaning "all's well." They wrote:

Sage helps the nerves, and by its powerful might, Palsy is cured and fever put to flight!

Today, scientists know that sage is a natural preservative. It also stops people from sweating too much. In Europe today, doctors suggest sage gargles for people with sore throats.

Rosemary

Rosemary is a woody shrub with needle-shaped leaves. In the Middle Ages it was known as a love potion. If someone was tapped with a rosemary flower, they thought the person would fall in love.

According to medieval wisdom, a sprig of rosemary tucked under a pillow would keep bad dreams away. Planted in a garden, it would repel witches. (It must come in handy on Hallowe'en!)

Rosemary water — a sprig covered with water in a bottle — is a nice skin refresher. Knights used it as aftershave, and ladies splashed it on their faces in hot weather for a refreshing, "Ahhhh!"

Will Rosemary Preserve a Potato?

Rosemary contains a strong anti-oxidant, which is a kind of preservative that stops oxygen from oxidizing, which causes damage. (Rust comes from oxidation, for example.) Modern doctors say that stopping oxidation inside our bodies — by eating anti-oxidants — can help us stay healthy.

To prove (or disprove!) the power of rosemary, slice a potato in half. Leave one side alone, in the open air. Rub the other side with crushed rosemary leaves, and leave it alone, too.

Check the potatoes in an hour or two. Does rosemary slow the process of the potato turning black?

The End of Medieval Times

How did the days of knights and castles come to an end? The answer is that it happened slowly and gradually. Little by little, the tight, enclosed world of the village or town opened up and gave way to the wider world of discovery.

❖ **The Hundred Years' War,**
❖ **a terrible disease,**
❖ **the invention of guns,**
❖ **a friendly saint, and**
❖ **an Italian traveler**

All of the above played a part in the end of the Middle Ages. Read on to see what finally happened.

EXTREMELY OUTRAGEOUS! THE HUNDRED YEARS' WAR

Imagine a fight that goes on and on, spinning around like a dizzy carousel. That's what the Hundred Years' War between England and France was like. The war was fought at the end of the Middle Ages, from 1337 to 1453. (Use subtraction to find out how many years the war actually lasted.)

After more than a century of fighting, the Hundred Years' War left everyone fed up and sick of battle!

THE WORST OF THE WORST

The bubonic (bew-BON-ik) plague, or Black Death, was a horrible contagious disease that contributed to the end of the Middle Ages by destroying more than a third of all the people in Europe in just one year. The disease was carried by fleas that lived on rats and other animals. The deaths caused a shortage of workers. From then on, if nobles wanted goods and services, they had to pay their former serfs and peasants for them. As common people started gaining wealth, feudalism gradually came to an end.

THE SECRET OF RING AROUND THE ROSY

When you were little, you probably played Ring Around the Rosy, as kids have for the past thousand years. But did you know that the words of that innocent little sing-song have a deeper, darker meaning?

That's because Ring Around the Rosy comes from the days of the Black Death.

"Ring Around the Rosy" stands for a traditional dance with everyone holding hands and marching around a tree in a circle.

"Pocket full of posey" stands for the flowers people carried in their pockets to cover up the awful smell of the sores caused by the disease.

"Ashes, ashes" stands for the piles of bodies that had to be burned so that more people wouldn't be infected.

"All fall down," as you can probably imagine, stands for people dying!

Now how did that sad tale of the bubonic plague become a popular nursery rhyme?

What Ignorance Can Do

Jewish people had a hard time in the Middle Ages because of intolerance. Jews (and women and people of color) were not allowed to own property. They had to live in special neighborhoods, called ghettos (GET-toes).

But a strange thing happened during the Black Death. The Jews did not get sick. Unfortunately, instead of being happy for them, some people claimed that the Jews had poisoned the water wells of the sick! This idea spread more hate and fear.

Can you guess the real reason that Jewish people didn't get the plague? The Jewish people were forced to live apart from other people, so they didn't catch the contagious disease.

The End of the Middle Ages

The invention of guns helped to end the feudal system, too. A sword or lance is no match for firearms, and firing a gun requires much less skill than shooting an arrow. Skilled knights and archers were put out of business in a very short time.

WIDER HORIZONS

Merchants, explorers, and traders accumulated money and knowledge. These travelers brought back new ideas and inventions from all over the world. By the early 1300s, the simple — and often backward — ways of towns and villages didn't satisfy people anymore. They saw that there was more to life, a greater world than they had ever dreamed of back in medieval times.

TWO POPES AND DISHONORABLE KNIGHTS

Over time, with all the fighting, the Code of Chivalry could not prevent knights and nobles from stealing and killing wherever they went.

Then, the Church split in half, with two different popes — and even three — claiming to be the head of Christians everywhere. With both the nobility and the Church weakened, power began shifting to the common people.

Questions Questions

Do you think it is fair to judge people by where they live?

❖

Do you think it is better or worse for different kinds of people to try to live together?

❖

If only the same kind of people live together, will it make it easier or harder to understand others?

❖

Do you think it is interesting, or scary, to meet different kinds of people?

❖

What's it like where you live? Are all the people one color or one religion? If so, how will you meet other kinds of people?

Think About It:

With the invention of guns, knights were suddenly unemployed. What a major change! But, unfortunately, inventing "better" weapons didn't stop there. Today, weapons of destruction boggle the mind. Do you think a country's having violent weapons prevents war or causes war?

Marco Polo, the Great 'Milione'✢

"I was just a boy of fourteen years when I went on my adventures. My uncle, my father, and I traveled a million miles," said Marco Polo, the famous merchant of Venice. His beard was streaked with gray, but when he spoke of his trip to Asia, his dark eyes twinkled like a child's.

Polo was standing in the town square of Venice with a small crowd around him. "We met a million people in foreign lands, and saw a million strange sights!"

"A million this, a million that," muttered Luigi to his friend, Mario. The two were fishermen who had stopped to listen.

"We went all the way east, to the land of Cathay. I became an advisor to Kublai Kahn, the great Mongol leader," Polo continued. "He was rich! So rich! He had a million rubies in a bowl. They were just sitting there looking beautiful. 'Do you like them, Marco?' he asked me. 'Then take some!' And here they are!"

Polo pulled two beautiful red gems from his pocket and held them up for the crowd to see.

"He could have bought those rubies right here in Venice," Luigi snickered.

"But maybe he's telling the truth," Mario suggested.

"Oh, I saw amazing things, my friends," the old man went on. "I traveled across a vast desert — a million miles long at least. There, at night, with my own eyes and ears, I saw and heard spirits singing! A million spirits, and they sang so beautifully that I cried."

"Rubies, free for the taking? Desert spirits that sing?" muttered Luigi. "What a liar this guy is."

"In one strange land, a man took a piece of cloth and put it into a blazing fire. But the cloth did not burn — not one little bit!"

With that, a buzz went through the crowd. Even the people who wanted to believe Marco were sure that cloth always burned.

"In Kublai Kahn's court, there are no coins. All over his land they used small pieces of paper as money," the merchant continued. "When I wanted to buy something, I gave the merchant paper, and he gave me whatever I wanted in return."

Luigi shook his head in disgust. "Now I know he is lying for sure! How could people do business with no coins! Besides, who would sit and write all the little papers. It just doesn't make sense."

But his friend looked more thoughtful. "Maybe the lands of the East are very different from our own land, Luigi," Mario suggested.

"Spirits singing in the desert? Cloth that doesn't burn? Money made of paper? Don't tell me you are falling for this ridiculous story!"

"We saw men with tails like dogs, but the most amazing thing ..." Marco was saying, with a look of wonder on his grizzled face. "The Kublai Kahn let people pray to any god at all. As long as they obeyed his laws, they were free to worship however they wished! In Kublai Kahn's land, there were a million different ideas about God and religion."

"That's the last straw," Luigi muttered to his friend Mario. Then he straightened his body and raised his hands to get attention. "Hey you, Marco Polo!" he shouted. "I'm going to call you 'Il Milione' from now on! Because you tell a million lies! No king would ever allow people to worship any god they wanted! Spirits don't sing in the desert, and cloth has to burn if you put it in fire! As for the idea of paper money, how did you dream up such nonsense!"

Marco Polo looked hurt. Then he shrugged his shoulders, and said quietly, "I did not tell half of what I saw."

✢'Milione' means millions in Italian

Was Marco Polo a Liar or Truth Teller? You Decide.

Scholars are still arguing about whether Marco Polo told the truth about his journeys. His enthusiastic telling of the stories was full of exaggeration, that's for sure. Some say he traveled only halfway to Cathay (modern China) and that some of his written adventures were stories that other merchants had told him.

Here's a list of the outrageous claims in his stories. Do you think they are true or false?

❖ **Marco said he traveled "a million miles."**

That's an exaggeration for sure! The whole earth is only 25,000 miles around.

❖ **Marco said the Kublai Khan was very rich.**

The Khan was the Emperor of the Mongols, the fearless warlike people who conquered China in Polo's day. His wealth was legendary.

❖ **Marco said he saw and heard spirits singing in the desert.**

The Takla Makan Desert, north of Tibet, is famous for the musical sounds of its sand. The scientific explanation is that shifting sands, dunes, and falling sand cliffs echo all over the desert. As for the spirits he saw, they were probably mirages caused by heat waves.

❖ **Marco said he saw cloth that did not catch fire.**

The cloth could have been made of asbestos, the fire retardant.

❖ **Marco said paper was used as money.**

That's absolutely true. But the funny thing is that Marco had no curiosity about the process of printing the money, or why the money was valuable. He seemed to think that the Khan just made money up to please himself.

❖ **Marco said there were men with tails like dogs.**

This is probably a big fat whopper. He probably got the story from someone else, who got it from someone else, who got it from.... well, you know how that goes!

❖ **Marco Polo said men could be tolerant of others' religions and differences.**

What a surprise to people of the Middle Ages, and yet, it's surely the way we live today!

IL MILIONE

Marco Polo was nicknamed "Il Milione" because of his tales. But one thing is certain, when Johannes Gutenberg made a printing press, Polo's book *The Description of the World* caused the people to open their minds and encouraged "millions" of new possibilities!

THE MAGNA CARTA

In 1215 A.D., the English barons formed an alliance that forced the king to sign a "great charter," or the Magna Carta. This great charter gave no real rights to peasants or other common folk, but it did limit the king's power for the first time. At last, the king and queen were under the control of a very powerful law which said that trials were required before punishment, and taxes would be levied in a fairer manner. Perhaps this was the beginning of today's democracy!

THE PRINTING PRESS

With the invention of the printing press in the 1400s, books became available to one and all. It was this invention that totally changed the medieval world. Now, even common people could get knowledge — and KNOWLEDGE IS POWER! Common people began to take part in politics and the shaping of society.

With books, people rediscovered the ancient Greek and Roman cultures and found out that there were great civilizations other than their own.

By the end of the Middle Ages, the world had widened and deepened. The lights of learning that had gone out all over Europe were being lit once again, and creative thinking and new ideas began to flourish.

The Middle Ages gave way and the rebirth, or Renaissance, began.

Visions of the Future

There were also people who had visions of the technological future, even then. Here's what Sir Francis Bacon wrote in the 1200s: "Cars can be made so that without animals, people will move with unbelievable rapidity." He sure got that right, didn't he?

Traces of the Past

The Middle Ages came to an end about 500 years ago. But traveler, your eagle eyes will find traces of the past all around you, even today, if you look around to find them!

Then & Now

Hunt for Castles, Banners, and Flags

Look around. Notice buildings that resemble castles. Watch for flags and banners. Businesses sometimes use knights and castles in ads.

Take a moment to look up the names "Castle" and "Knight" in a phone book. Any trace of the past there?

Go on a castle-time hunt in a stack of old magazines. Look for pictures of royalty, stained-glass windows, Valentine hearts, and more. What evidence of the Middle Ages do you find where you live?

FARE THEE WELL!

Well, traveler, now that you've explored the Middle Ages, you can keep the best and get rid of the rest. Learning about these dark days can show us how great our own times really are. As citizens of our time, we have rich possibilities that people didn't have back then. Learning about the feudal system reminds us of the opportunity we have to make our lives fuller, happier, more accepting, and more democratic.

There's lots of stuff that we can keep from those sometimes merry but mostly murky old days, too. It's still fun to "divine" from nature, to create art and crafts, to sing, and put on plays. Using herbs will help us to stay healthy, and wassailing a tree now and then connects us to something that's very deep and very true inside us and out, in any age.

So wassail, wassail! Keep the spirit of well-being going!

Bibliography

Berresford Ellis, Peter. *The Druids.* Constable and Company Limited, 1994.

Bodo, Murray. *The Way of St. Francis.* Doubleday, 1984.

Boorstin, Daniel J. *The Discoverers.* Random House, 1983.

Brightling, Geoff, Dann Brightling, Goeff Brightling, and Andrew Langley. *Medieval Life.* Eyewitness Books, Knopf, 1996.

Briquebec, John. *The Middle Ages Barbarian Invasions, and Medieval Europe.* Warwick Press, 1990.

Bunson, Matthew. *The Encyclopedia of the Middle Ages.* Facts on File, 1995.

Corbishly, Mike. *The Medieval World.* Peter Bedrick Books, 1993.

Corrick, Jansa. *The Late Middle Ages.* Lucent Books, 1995.

Demi. *The Adventures of Marco Polo.* Holt Reinhart Winston, 1982.

Gee, Robin. *Living in Castle Times.* Usborne, 1982.

Gregory, Tony. *The Dark Ages.* Facts on File, 1993.

Kenyon, Sherrilyn. *The Writer's Guide to Everyday Life in the Middle Ages.* Writer's Digest Books, 1995.

MacDonald, Fiona. *The Middle Ages.* Facts on File, 1993.

Mason, Anthony. *The Middle Ages If You Were There.* Simon & Schuster Books, 1996.

Miquel, Pierre, and Pierre Probst. *The Days of Knights & Castles.* Silver Burdett Company, 1980.

Morgan, Gwyneth. *Life in a Medieval Village.* Cambridge University Press, 1982.

Oakes, Catherine. *Exploring the Middle Ages.* Harcourt Brace Jovanovich, 1989.

O'Neil, Richard. *The Middle Ages.* Crescent Books, 1992.

Rowling, Marjorie. *Everyday Life in Medieval Times.* Dorset Press, 1987.

Rugoff, Milton. *Marco Polo's Adventures in China.* New York: American Heritage Publishing Company, 1964.

Scarre, Christopher, Ed. *Smithsonian Timeliness of the Ancient World.* Smithsonian Institution, 1993.

Tuchman, Barbara Wertheim. *A Distant Mirror: The Calamitous 14th Century.* Knopf, 1978.

Index

More Good Books from Williamson Publishing

Please see last page for ordering information.

KALEIDOSCOPE KIDS® Books

Kaleidoscope Kids® books for children ages 7 to 14 are 96 pages, fully illustrated, 10 x 10, $12.95 US/$19.95 CAN.

THE LEWIS & CLARK EXPEDITION
Join the Corps of Discovery to Explore Uncharted Territory
by Carol A. Johmann

ANCIENT ROME!
Exploring the Culture, People & Ideas of This Powerful Empire
by Avery Hart and Sandra Gallagher

ForeWord Magazine Book of the Year Finalist
Teachers' Choice Award
SKYSCRAPERS!
Super Structures to Design & Build
by Carol A. Johmann

Children's Book Council Notable Book
WHO REALLY DISCOVERED AMERICA?
Unraveling the Mystery & Solving the Puzzle
by Avery Hart

Children's Book Council Notable Book
Dr. Toy 10 Best Educational Products
PYRAMIDS!
50 Hands-On Activities to Experience Ancient Egypt
by Avery Hart and Paul Mantell

Children's Book Council Notable Book
American Bookseller Pick of the Lists
KNIGHTS & CASTLES
50 Hands-On Activities to Experience the Middle Ages
by Avery Hart and Paul Mantell

American Bookseller Pick of the Lists
Parent's Guide Children's Media Award
ANCIENT GREECE!
40 Hands-On Activities to Experience This Wondrous Age
by Avery Hart and Paul Mantell

American Bookseller Pick of the Lists
¡MEXICO!
40 Activities to Experience Mexico Past and Present
by Susan Milord

Benjamin Franklin Silver Award
GOING WEST!
Journey on a Wagon Train to Settle a Frontier Town
by Carol A. Johmann and Elizabeth J. Rieth

Parents' Choice Recommended
BRIDGES!
Amazing Structures to Design, Build & Test
by Carol A. Johmann and Elizabeth J. Rieth

Teachers' Choice Award
GEOLOGY ROCKS!
50 Hands-On Activities to Explore the Earth
by Cindy Blobaum

THE BEAST IN YOU!
Activities & Questions to Explore Evolution
by Marc McCutcheon

Williamson's *KIDS CAN!*® Books

Kids Can!® books for children ages 6 to 14 are 128 to 176 pages, fully illustrated, 11 x 8 , $12.95 US/$19.95 CAN.

Parents' Choice Recommended
THE KIDS' BOOK OF WEATHER FORECASTING
Build a Weather Station, "Read" the Sky & Make Predictions!
with meteorologist Mark Breen and Kathleen Friestad

Parents' Choice Honor Award
THE KIDS' NATURAL HISTORY BOOK
Making Dinos, Fossils, Mammoths & More
by Judy Press

Parents' Choice Honor Award
American Institute of Physics Science Writing Award
GIZMOS & GADGETS
Creating Science Contraptions that Work (& Knowing Why)
by Jill Frankel Hauser

Parents' Choice Recommended
KIDS' ART WORKS!
Creating with Color, Design, Texture & More
by Sandi Henry

Parents Magazine Parents' Pick
Real Life Award
KIDS LEARN AMERICA!
Bringing Geography to Life with People, Places & History
by Patricia Gordon and Reed C. Snow

REAL-WORLD MATH for Hands-On Fun!
by Cindy A. Littlefield

American Bookseller Pick of the Lists
Benjamin Franklin Best Juvenile Nonfiction Award
SUPER SCIENCE CONCOCTIONS
50 Mysterious Mixtures for Fabulous Fun
by Jill Frankel Hauser

American Bookseller Pick of the Lists
Parents' Choice Approved
SUMMER FUN!
60 Activities for a Kid-Perfect Summer
by Susan Williamson

Selection of Book-of-the-Month; Scholastic Book Clubs
KIDS COOK!
Fabulous Food for the Whole Family
by Sarah Williamson and Zachary Williamson

Parents' Choice Gold Award
Benjamin Franklin Best Juvenile Nonfiction Award
KIDS MAKE MUSIC!
Clapping and Tapping from Bach to Rock
by Avery Hart and Paul Mantell

Parents' Choice Approved
Parent's Guide Children's Media Award
BOREDOM BUSTERS!
The Curious Kids' Activity Book
by Avery Hart and Paul Mantell

The Kids' Guide to FIRST AID
All about Bruises, Burns, Stings, Sprains & Other Ouches
by Karen Buhler Gale, R.N.